AMAZON SELLING SECRETS

How to Make $1K-$10K a Month
Selling Your Own Products on Amazon

William U. Peña, MBA

*Amazon Selling Secrets: How to Make $1K-$10K a Month
Selling Your Own Products on Amazon*

www.Amazonsellingsecretsbook.com

First printing 2014

ISBN-13: 978-1500123680

ISBN-10: 1500123684

Contents

Introduction

Successful Selling on Amazon— An Overview

This book is designed to give you a system that will provide you with an extra $1,000 to $10,000 a month in passive income by selling your own products on Amazon. By putting to practice the principles and the practical steps that I share in this book, you'll be able to generate a second income, that can either supplement or replace your current income. Even more, Amazon provides you so many great resources, which will allow you to be able to create a second income working less than ten hours a month.

The idea is that you are going to learn how to utilize the many automated systems, technology, and resources provided by Amazon in order to sell and make money, yet using very little of your own resources. And, even though this type of business does require you to take care of customers, the best part is that those customers are going to reward you. They will reward you in abundant sales, profits, referrals, as well as the good feeling that you get from servicing all different types people.

Now, one thing this book is not, is that it's not a get rich quick scheme. It will take work. But the best part about the work is, that once you get it under your belt, you don't necessarily have to do it anymore. The system will do all the work for you.

Also, this book will not make you a million dollars. But, it will provide you with a means toward financial independence. This system is designed to show you how to make a passive, residual monthly income to either replace your current active income, or just to add multiple streams of income to what you're already doing. And, if you continue with the principles that we talk about in this book, successfully selling your own products on Amazon, and then taking this system and expanding on it, there's no reason why you can't make a million dollars.

I'm sure you've heard a lot of things about selling on Amazon. Yet, this book is not about retail arbitrage. Retail arbitrage is just the fancy way of saying to "buy low and then sell high." And you've probably seen a lot of people scrambling at different discount thrift stores trying to buy things and then try to sell them on Amazon. This is not what this book is about. The reason I'm saying this is that there is a specific reason why selling your own products, with your own brand (also known as private labeling), is a lot more lucrative and a lot less work than actually going out and trying to sell someone else's product.

Specifically, the profits with retail arbitrage are generally very low. You do a lot of work in order just to make a little bit of money, but then shipping costs, and other costs tend to eat up all your profits. The best part about what we're going to talk about in this book is that instead of the small profit margins you get with retail arbitrage; by selling your own products, you can expect a return on investment of 100, 200, even 500 percent. This is because when you sell your own products with your own brand name, you'll be able to consistently create enough value that you can charge very high prices for your products.

Now if you are anything like me, you're probably thinking, "Am I going to have to hold a ton of inventory in my home?" The answer is no. You don't have to. Because Amazon provides you with great solutions for this, so that you will never have to store inventory in your own home ever again.

So if this sounds good to you, strap yourself in and get ready for an exciting ride through the jungles of Amazon...

CHAPTER 1

How to Successfully Sell Your Own Products on Amazon

Now, what does it take in order to be successful at selling products on Amazon? Here is an overview of the Amazon Sales Success System, and what you will learn in this book:

1. **Identifying Desirable Products**—You will learn how to find great products that people will be eager to buy.

2. **Creating A Unique Brand**—You will learn how to take any generic product and add a very powerful brand to it, and create a substantial amount of value that people want to pay for.

3. **Finding High Quality Product Sources**—You are going to learn how to find great places where you can source high quality products to sell on Amazon.

4. **Creating High Converting Amazon Listings**—Once you list your product on Amazon, the way you convey your message will

1

influence your buyers in a very big way. Your listing will really determine whether they're going to buy from you or not and also the type of prices that you charge for your products as well. You will learn how to write the most emotionally compelling listing that will compel people to buy.

5. **Creating The Most Profit Possible**—You are going to learn how to price your products the right way, and how to minimize your expenses but still maintain a high quality product, that produces a great profit.

6. **Testing And Validating Your Product**—Just because you find a product, doesn't mean people are going to buy it. You are going to learn how to test your product in the Amazon marketplace to make sure that you find the product that you will be able to sell a lot of, and make big profit from.

7. **Effectively Fulfilling Orders And Managing Your Inventory**—You will also learn how to fulfill your orders to customers and manage your inventory in such a way that it creates a constant, efficient stream of income from your business. Also you will learn how to get your system so well dialed in that you really don't do that much work in order to make it work.

8. **Providing Outstanding Customer Satisfaction**—In Amazon, customer satisfaction is critical, especially because Amazon is known for their outstanding customer satisfaction. You will learn how to stay in alignment with that idea, and how to get Amazon customers to continuously purchase from you over and over again.

9. **Getting Abundant Reviews**—The Holy Grail in Amazon is the ability to get abundant reviews. The value comes from creating social proof that will motivate people to want to buy your products. You are going to learn how to get abundant four and five star reviews that will increase the value of your product.

10. **Automating Your Amazon Business**—You will learn how to use the tools you will have at your disposal to be able to cut down the amount of time, effort, resources, and money you spend, but still continue to get a large profit.

11. **Growing your Amazon Selling Business**—You are going to learn special ways to grow your Amazon Selling Business, so that you'll be able to not just make $10,000 a month but even $100,000 a month and more.

Expectations

Before we get started, I want to talk to you about what you should realistically expect in following the Amazon Selling system in this book. It's always important to know exactly what to expect, whether good or bad, so that you'll be able to have the best success possible.

So, what are some realistic expectations that you should have about trying to sell your own products on Amazon?. Generally, it starts with first understanding what your timeframe looks like. You can realistically expect that it will take you about three to six months to start seeing a profit. Now, you can make a profit much sooner than that, and I personally have made profit the first six weeks from when I started following the steps in this system. But a realistic expectation is it will take you about three months to start seeing a profit, so be prepared for it.

Next, you will need some capital in order to get started. I would suggest that you obtain $1,000 to $2,000, in order for it to be the smoothest ride possible for you. Now, the good news is that you don't need that entire $1,000 to $2,000 all at once (I actually started with $200). And you will make more money and profit selling products, that you can reinvest into the business to help with your expenses. But, generally, if you start with access to capital, then the process becomes a whole lot easier. Again, it doesn't have to be your money; it can be somebody else's or it could be credit. The idea is that you start with some form of capital.

Another expectation you should have is that there will be a learning curve, just like you would expect in learning anything new. So, be patient with yourself. It will take time. As entrepreneurs, I know we can be a bit impatient if we don't see results right away. But the one thing that you can guarantee, is that since you're going to be learning something new, then things will not always go the way you expect. Just make sure that you're ready for it by giving yourself the patience and the space to be able to learn from the process.

Also, expect to wait a while to see results. The reason I share this is because, if you're an entrepreneur like me, you probably don't like to wait. Yet, there is a lot of waiting in this Amazon Selling business. It could be waiting for suppliers to get back to you. Or, sometimes you will test different products and you will have to wait to see how customers respond, etc. Just be prepared to do some waiting. In other words, you're going to put out a lot of fishing lines out, but you have to wait to actually catch the fish.

Last, you will be working with vendors overseas. Specifically in this book, I'm going to talk about working with vendors and wholesale suppliers from China. So get ready for a bit of a culture shock if you haven't dealt with companies in China before. Be prepared to deal with people from a completely different culture, and different language. They think differently too, so you have to be very patient with them.

Rewards

Now let's discuss some of the rewards that you can expect from putting this Amazon Selling System to practice. First, you can expect to start making a minimum of $1,000 to $5,000 in profit in the first three to six months. This is actually quite common, and this has been my experience also.

You can also expect to make five to six figures in the first year that you start this business. This was my experience as well. A lot of other people who follow this Amazon Selling process, and follow all the steps that I share with you in this book, typically make five figures to six figures in their first year. Some even make seven figures because of the kind of time and effort they put into it.

The last reward, and the reward that I appreciate most about this type of business, is that once you get the system down, it only takes about one to two hours a day to work this business. I'll even talk about some ways to further automate your business, so that you can actually spend even less time than that.

Getting Started Selling on Amazon

The first step to start selling on Amazon, is that you will need to open an Amazon Seller Central Account. This is Amazon's web portal, where you manage your products, payments and everything else in your Amazon Selling business.

To sign up, you first need to go to www.amazon.com/sellonamazon, and you will be given a choice to open either an Individual Account for free (you get charged $.99 for each sale), or a Professional account for $40 a month (with no per sale charge). If you are just starting out, an Individual Account is probably the way to go, since you are only charged $.99 for every product you sell, and no other fee. Once you are selling over 40 orders per month you can switch to the Professional Account and receive the extra benefits that come from it.

The steps for opening an Amazon Seller Central Account are pretty straight forward. Just go to www.amazon.com/sellonamazon pick the Individual Sellers Account and fill out the form you are given. Here are a few items they will ask you for, and that you will need to have ready to open your account:

1. Legal Name—this is your business name, DBA name, or your personal name if you are doing business as an individual.
2. Business Address—your official business address.
3. Credit Card Number—in case Amazon needs to charge you for anything.
4. Bank Account Number—to deposit your payments.
5. Display Name (or Brand Name)—the name of your Brand.
6. Logo—(optional) to help brand your Amazon store.
7. Set up shipping rates—If you want to offer free shipping on your items this is where you make the changes.

CHAPTER

2

Identifying Products That Sell

Now let's talk about the first part of the Amazon selling process, identifying a desirable product. How do you find the best type of products that people will want to buy? Well, it takes three things:

1. **Establishing the right product criteria.** This means creating a list of specific criteria that will help you find the most successful product. You need a way to filter products, because not only do you want to find a bestselling product, but you also want to do it with the least amount of expense. You also want to make sure that your customers are satisfied because of the high quality of the product. So, by setting up the best product criteria first, you'll have a better chance finding the ideal product.

2. **Finding the hottest selling products on the Amazon Bestseller List.** I am going to show you exactly how to go on Amazon, look at their list of bestselling products, and then find the

perfect products that fit all of your criteria. You will also find the best generic products that you can transform with branding and packaging, in order to create your own products.

3. **Picking the Best Product Timing.** Product timing refers to finding the best time to produce your product. There are a lot of seasons and holidays that influence how popular a product will be. So, we will discuss how to identify the proper product timing to give your product the best chance at success.

Establishing the Best Product Criteria

You need to be able to pick the best product criteria that will guarantee the most success of your Amazon selling business. This is the "strategic planning" part of your Amazon business.

Now, you could jump on Amazon right now, see what the best sellers are, pick some products, source and sell them, and then fall flat on your face. Why? Because even though you did all the work, you didn't foresee the challenges that could come up because you picked the wrong product, picked the wrong product category, or the timing was wrong.

So, what I want to do is give you a general overview of some good product criteria that can help you have the best chance at finding and successfully selling products on Amazon:

1. **Weight**—You're going to be have these products shipped to you from other places, and you're also going to ship them to customers as well. When you ship these products you want to make sure that you won't lose all your profit on shipping fees. In order to reduce shipping costs substantially, it's generally

best to have most of the products that you sell be under 5 pounds.

Personally, I try to only sell products that are under 3 pounds, but 5 pounds is the max for me. Now, the other benefit of this is that there are shipping companies, (I.e. FedEx, UPS, DHL, etc.) that have special discounts for products under a certain weight, so you could go up as high as 10 pounds, and still spend little on shipping.

2. **Liability**—It's best to minimize liability as much as possible. So stay away from anything that has any type of risk potential. I don't sell wood stoves, for obvious reasons. Those could turn around and actually hurt the customer and the customer could come back and sue me. I also try to avoid baby products. In other words, anything that could potentially cause people harm, I generally stay away from.

My motto is that as long as you eliminate the liability problem, then you never have to worry about it. Again, the goal is to create a passive business with the least amount of time, effort, resource, and money; and selling high liability products can jeopardize this tremendously.

3. **Price**—I generally try to find products that I can sell between $20 and $200. Personally, I tend to go after higher priced products because I try to create enough of a valuable brand that people can justify spending a lot for it. But a $20 product can be just as good, especially if it only cost you a couple of dollars to produce. And if a large group of people buy them, you can create a very lucrative business for yourself.

4. **Size**—I also try to find products that are small in size. Why? Because they're easy to pack, and easy to ship. Try to avoid odd shaped products, even if they are light. If you find a lightweight product but it's long, like a tennis racket, then you're going to find it difficult to find packaging for it.

5. **Minimal Moving Parts**—I also try to find products with minimal moving parts. Why? Because the more moving parts you have, the greater the chance the product has for breaking down. Then, the more chances you have of your customer coming back to you and asking for a refund. So, try to avoid those too.

6. **Generic**—For your Amazon selling business, you are going to focus on products that are very generic in nature. This is because the more generic they are, the easier you can add your own brand, your logo, and make slight changes to the product so that it becomes a unique product that is your own. Then, after that, you can pretty much charge whatever you want as long as you can show people the value that the product has in their lives. Generic products are the products I will be focusing on mostly in this book.

7. **Easy to Source**—This means high quality items that you can find many suppliers for. If you find a great product, but no suppliers, then you've wasted your time. Or If you find a great product but very few suppliers for it, then you are at the mercy of whatever your supplier charges you. You want to find products that you can find multiple suppliers for so that you can negotiate the best rates for your product. Later on in this book, I'm going to show you exactly how to do this.

Additional Product Criteria—What to Avoid

Now, there are some additional criteria you can use to help you find great products. For example, you want to focus on products that have an established following. Meaning, that it has some type of niche. Generally, this includes some type of hobby or some type of emotional, meaningful, and desirable component to the product, that will more guarantee that you'll always have customers coming to buy from you. This is because these type of products cross over the boundary from what a customer needs to what a customer wants. The more emotional component the product has, the more of an impulse buy the customer will make. And of course, this also gives you the ability to charge higher prices because people, when they're emotional, tend to make decisions based on what's going to make them feel good. And hey, if that means splurging, they'll do it as well, which is better for you.

Just to give you an idea of some of my own personal criteria, here is a list of things that I generally avoid:

1. **Electronics**—I generally don't do electronics. Now, you can do electronics. But for me, it goes against my rule of a lot of moving parts. This is because, when you have electronics you 1) have people constantly returning things and 2) with electronics it's really hard to determine the quality of the product, when you're working with overseas sources. So for me, electronics are out.

2. **Clothing**—I generally stay away from clothing. I don't want to have to deal with sizes, different colors, or other variations.

3. **Expiration Date**—I avoid any products that can expire, like consumables or any type of product whose quality diminishes rapidly with time (I.e. natural products, makeup, etc.).

4. **Cell phones or cell phone accessories**—this is one of the most popular categories in Amazon, but also the one that is most saturated with competition. I generally try to stay away from it. Why? Because it's better to be a big fish in a small pond than to be a small fish in a big pond. And if you become a big enough fish in the small pond, later you can move to the bigger pond, but right now focus on being the big fish.

5. **Baby Products**—I avoid baby products for obvious reasons; too much potential liability for my taste.

6. **Popular Brands**—I avoid popular brands. Why? Because it's hard to brand something that everyone knows belongs to a major brand. For example, when you think of diapers who do you think about? You think of Pampers, you think of Huggies, etc. Yet, cloth diapers are more generic, and there's really not a big name for this industry, which would make it a great product to go after (Now, I would avoid cloth diapers because I avoid clothing, but it may be a good fit for you).

So generally I avoid popular brands. I try to go for the more generic brands. A good example would be a yoga mat. There's no big name for yoga mats, which makes it an ideal product to brand as your own. Find a great quality yoga mat, brand it, and sell it; next thing you know you create a great stream of income.

The Amazon Bestseller List— Shooting Fish in a Barrel

There is no better place to identify hot products than on the Amazon Best Seller List.

The best strategy to find hot products to sell, is to go through each major category on the Amazon Bestseller List looking for the products that meet the product criteria that you create.

I generally start looking for products in the Amazon Bestseller main categories, then I will go into subcategories. The best part of going into subcategories, is that you can find some really interesting, but profitable niches, with little competition, which you can later dominate.

Here are the steps that I take when I go through the Amazon best seller list searching for products:

1. Go to the Amazon Bestseller List. You can find it on this link: www.amazon.com/Best-Sellers/zgbs. Or do a search on Google for "Amazon Bestseller List" and you will easily find it.

2. On the left of the screen, you will find a list of main product categories. Choose a product category where you will find the most generic products that fit your criteria. This will usually include most categories, but generally I focus on the following:

   • Automotive (for their accessories).
   • Camera and Photo.
   • Home and Kitchen.
   • Home Improvement.

- Kitchen and Dining.

- Musical Instruments.

- Patio, Lawn and Garden.

- Pet supplies.

- Sports and Outdoors.

3. Open an excel file, and as you look for products through the main category that fit your product criteria, copy and paste product titles and prices into your excel file.

4. After you finish going through the main category, go through the subcategories and do the same (there are 100 products per category).

5. Then move on the next main category on the list (I'll usually go 3—4 categories deep).

6. When you are done going through the different main categories and subcategories, go through your list on excel, and choose 10 products you determine are the best out of the list. Start sourcing those first.

This process should result in helping you find 10—20 really great products that you can now begin to find suppliers for.

You now also have a whole list of products you can go back to, once you get your first products successfully selling, to look for new products to sell in the future.

Identifying Proper Product Timing

We mentioned before how some products tend to sell a lot more at certain times of the year than others. Valentines, Christmas, Easter, Mother's Day, are holidays or seasons that tend to motivate people emotionally to purchase. So, sometimes you have to ask yourself, "What product would be ideal to sell right now?

One of the first criteria for choosing the right product timing is your budget. If you don't have a lot of money to spend or you don't have a lot of capital or credit to use, you might want to focus on a lower priced product. For example, you could focus on a more valuable $50 product, that you can turn around and sell for $150, but if your budget's is limited you can only purchase a few, and only sell a few. On the other hand, if your budget is low, you can go after the 10 cent product and buy it in bulk, and then sell them for $10 each. All of a sudden you have 500 to 1,000 percent return. Granted, you won't make as much money as the higher priced product, but you're making enough profit that you can use later on to buy the more expensive product as well. So, the question you need to ask yourself is, "How much money do I have to spend right now?"

So, If your budget is low, stick to the lower priced products. If your budget is higher, feel free to go for the bigger products with the higher price tags.

Another good question to ask is, "Is it the right season for the product?" Though, it is best to pick products that are not dependent on any one season, you generally want to be aware of products whose product sales are greatly boosted because of the holidays. So, to get the best bang for your buck, try to pick products that can be influenced by seasons and holidays, the ones that give customers a big motivation to buy.

In other words, find products that make great gifts for the holidays. You could choose to sell the telescopic pool rake, but you have to understand that it may not make a great gift for the holidays. On the other hand, an extra thick yoga mat, or a yoga mat carry bag would make the perfect gift for the millions of people that are into yoga.

CHAPTER 3

Creating a Unique Brand—Part I

In this chapter we are going to talk about how to create a unique brand. The best way to describe what a brand is, is that a brand is the name and logo that inspires a specific feeling in your customers, that ultimately motivates them to buy. In other words, a brand creates so much value in the mind of your customers, that they will feel highly motivated to spend all types of money to buy your product.

To be clear, this entire book hinges on your ability to create a unique and valuable brand for your product. This is because you can have an incredibly outstanding product, but if customers aren't able to see the value, they won't purchase it. On the other hand, if you create a unique enough brand, and a unique enough experience in the customer's mind, they will be emotionally compelled to buy that product, and tell their friends about it. That is why in this book I focus more on selling your own products. You see, you can take a very generic product, add a powerful brand to it, and then all of a sudden you have people spending all kinds of money on your product.

So, let's look at a few different criteria that it takes to create a unique and valuable brand:

1. **Establishing a Unique Selling Proposition (USP)**—This is the one feature of your product that makes it unique, different, and better than everyone else's, so that customers will be willing to spend money on your product.

2. **Choosing the Ideal Name for Your Brand**—If you pick the right name for your brand, it can motivate people to feel good and to emotionally compel them to purchase your product.

3. **Designing the Ideal Logo.** The purpose of a logo is to choose the right image that puts the right perspective in the customer's mind, that will emotionally compel them to buy.

4. **Picking the Ideal Name for Your Product**—It creates a powerful experience for customers when a product has a name. It's not enough that the car is a Honda or a Toyota, but people appreciate it more if it's a Honda Pilot or Toyota Camry.

5. **Designing the Ideal Packaging.** Designing the ideal packaging is the difference between getting something in the mail wrapped in bubble wrap and then getting something in the mail with a very glossy, good looking box that makes you feel like, "Wow! I just bought something of value."

6. **Creating the Ideal Experience**—This includes creating the best experience for customers that puts them in the perfect

emotional state, that'll make it very easy for them to take out their credit cards and buy.

Establishing A Unique Selling Proposition (USP)

So how do you create a unique selling proposition for your product? Well, for every product, I first start by trying to find the answer to this question: "What will make my product different, unique, and better than everyone else's?"

Now, since we're working with a generic product, we want to make it stand out from everyone else's. Now, it doesn't have to be something that makes it better than everyone else's, it just needs to be unique. Because uniqueness create value in the mind of your customer.

In order to find a USP for my product, the first thing I like to do is to pick a particular feature of the product to work with. I start with a list of all of the different features and attributes of the product, and then I choose one specific feature that my competitors are not focusing on, that will be valuable to my customer. Then I turn that one unique feature into my unique selling proposition.

Once I find the feature that brings a lot of benefit to the customer, I use my branding to convey the benefit of that feature over and over. In other words, by picking a unique feature attribute and building on it, customers will remember that product for that one main thing, and it will become the one idea that brings the most value for them.

Now, a competitor could simply choose that feature also and make it their USP. Then you will be evenly matched with your competitor, and you will find yourself competing on price. A solution to this is to find a USP that is difficult to copy. And the more scarce your USP is, the more value your product will have to your customers also. This is known as your "competitive advantage."

You can make your features unique by asking your manufacturer to create a special design modification. Or you can make an agreement with your supplier to exclusively sell their product on Amazon. You can also add a special accessory, or a special design that your competitors cannot copy. The idea is that by choosing a scarce USP, you are creating a competitive advantage in the marketplace that competitors cannot copy. Also, the more unique and scarce it is, the more valuable it will be for your customer.

Finding a Great USP

So where do you go to find a great USP? One of the best places to start is to look at your competitors. You start by finding a competitor that is selling the generic product you are considering. Then you look at all of their reviews, focusing especially on the reviews that are three stars and below. Look at what their customers are saying, specifically focusing on what their customers are complaining about. Now they could be complaining about a missing component. Or maybe they wish the product came with a particular accessory.

When you hear a lot of people complaining about the same things, make a list of these complaints, and choose one of them to make your unique selling proposition. You already know your customers are looking for it, and you also know that your competition is lacking it; so, you can go ahead and pick that feature and make it your USP. Next thing you know, you will quickly stand out from your competition, and collect the lion's share of business.

Another great place to find a great USP, is look at the specifications of your product, also known as "the product specs." Focus on a specific attribute you think will be very valuable in the eyes of your customer, and that other competitors are not focusing on. Or choose a feature that can be used in another capacity, that no one has thought about yet.

For example, I found a bestselling item in the bake ware category called Silicone Baking Cups. What I found out when reading the reviews, is that many customers were using these silicone baking cup liners as Bento Lunch Box Liners. This is a great example of a product that was sold for one reason, but could be used for another. So, instead of selling these silicone liners for baking I would sell them as a Bento Lunch Box Liner, and simply call them "Bento Buddy Silicone Bento Lunch Box Liners."

Creating The Ideal Brand Name

You can turn a generic product into a unique brand that people will remember, by simply giving it the best brand name. The brand name not only conveys the products unique features and benefits, but it sends the message to the customer that it is a valuable product that can meet their needs.

But how does one go about picking a great name for your brand? Well it starts by first asking yourself the question, "What feeling or emotion do I want to convey to my customer when they think about my product?" Whatever that feeling is, it should give you an idea of what direction you want to go when you pick the name for your brand. For example, if you are selling fun pet toys, you want your brand name to be something that makes people think about pet's having fun. Something like, "Witty Kitty Pet Toys," or "Merry Jerry Pet Toys," even, "AniMotion Pet Toys," could work.

So your brand name should create the feeling for your customers that says you can meet their needs or fulfill their desires. And by doing so, you will attract hundreds of customers to buy more from you than your competitors.

You also want a brand name that will help highlight your product's unique selling proposition as well. For example, if the USP of your product is that it is environmentally safe, then make sure your brand has an element of this in the name that you choose. Looking at our pet toys example, a name like "Frolic Natural Pet Toys," will probably work wonders at helping your customers think "fun, and environmentally friendly."

Now, it's also best to pick a "general" brand name that highlights your unique selling proposition. Why general? Because you may later decide to sell multiple products or different lines of products through that same brand name. In order not to reinvent the wheel, you may want to choose a brand name that is flexible enough to give you that option. Again our "Frolic" pet toys name can also be used for pet furniture, pet clothes, even pet food.

The Quickest Way to Choose a Kick Butt Brand Name

The quickest way to find a great brand name, is to look at the competitors that are already selling similar products. As you look at their brand name, you must understand that they already put the time, the effort, even the money to come up with that great brand. Why not find a name that conveys the same message as theirs, but uses different words? This is where a Thesaurus comes in really handy.

Here are the steps you can use to choose a great brand name:

1. First take your competitor's brand name, and look up at that name in a Thesaurus.

2. Review the other words to see if there are other ways of conveying the exact same message, with a really cool sounding word, that will appeal to customers.

3. Test it out with others and see if they get the message you are trying to convey.

You'll be amazed at how many really great words pop up, which you can use for your brand name.

CHAPTER 4

Creating a Unique Brand—Part II

Designing the Ideal Logo

A great brand also requires a great logo. And just like a great brand conveys a valuable message to the customer, so a great logo confirms that message.

So, you want to choose colors, fonts, and a design, that will lead the customer to emotionally connect with your brand and unique selling proposition. For example, if your brand name is Frolic Pet Toys, you want to pick colors that are compatible with that band. Light colors like: white, light blue, yellow, green (nature), etc., will work great. On the other hand, you want to stay away from dark colors like black, grey, or dark brown, because they have the opposite effect on the customer.

The idea behind this, is that just like people are influenced by words and pictures, people are influenced by colors and visual designs also.

Now, if you're like me, you may be thinking, "I don't have an artistic bone in my body!" or "I don't know what colors to choose!" This is where you can go to a place like Fiverr.com or Elance.com and find an affordable graphic designer to design your logo for you. You can give them your brand name, your USP and any other information that will help them design a great logo. You can even send them a couple of examples of competitor logos that you really like and see what they come up with. For best results, pay $5 each to three graphic designers on Fiverr.com and have them all design a logo for you. When you receive all three, pick the best one.

Now the logo they come up with doesn't have to look pretty to you. What's more important is that it looks pretty to your customers. Also, since you are probably going to test that logo to see if it appeals to your customers, it's probably best that you don't get too emotionally attached to it.

Coming Up With a Valuable Product Name

How about the product name itself? How do you pick a unique product name that will add even more value to your product? Well, again, the value is found in uniqueness. Just like your USP, the more unique the product name you choose, the more valuable it will be, and the higher the price you can charge.

There is a reason that car companies give cars names. A Toyota Camry, or a Honda Pilot is a lot more valuable than a car named, "The beige Toyota that is parked over there." And just like cars, once you give a product its own unique name, the sticker price can increase by thousands of dollars.

Before we said that we want our brand name to be general, because you're probably going to sell a bunch of products under it.

On the other hand, you want your product name to be as specific as possible, highlighting qualities that build on the product's benefits.

So how do you come up with great product names? I always say start by focusing on a specific product name that will highlight that product's USP. Another place to start is to look at what your competitors are doing. See what they're calling their products then use a thesaurus to get multiple variations of that name. Then test it with your product and see how people respond.

Choosing the Ideal Product Packaging

Just like your brand and your logo, your packaging should also highlight your unique selling proposition. For example if your brand and pet toy product name is "The Frolic Tuffball," you're not going to put it in a black box with silver words on it. It just won't give it the right feeling. Rather, a nice green and white box with a picture of a boy throwing a "Frolic Tuffball," as a golden retriever chases after it, in the park, on a sunny day, will probably highlight the USP best.

Again, the easiest place to look for great packaging ideas is your competitors. See what they're doing and try to do something similar, but make it unique to what you your unique selling proposition is. As for the actual box or container you will use, look at what your competitors use. You can copy the type of box or container they use, just change the labeling on it with your brand name, product name logo and colors.

This is where Fiverr.com and Elance.com come to the rescue, again. You can hire a package designer for as low as five bucks. For example, I hired someone at Fiverr.com to design the packaging for one of my products, and I was completely blown away by what they designed. For only five bucks, I got the most incredible package box that I am using to this day. I even gave the guy an extra five dollars because he did such a great design.

Just a quick note, you don't want to make the packaging too unique so it will be too expensive to produce. What I mean is, that you don't want to design packaging that is some strange shape that will cost you an arm and a leg to produce, You'll just end up using all your profits to pay for your packaging, and then you'll be out of business very quickly.

For printing your packaging you can always go to a printing company or a package printing company to produce them. There are places online that can produce packaging really well. In fact, many packaging companies have startup packages for new businesses at affordable prices.

Inserts, (the inside of the packaging) also make a difference. What I mean is, if you have a great package outside, you open it up, and it's garbage on the inside, it will take away from the value of the product. So avoid bubble wrap as much as you can. Crinkle cut filler actually looks nice, kraft or colored. Vacuform plastic works too because it maintains the shape of the particular product so you can just neatly put the product in there. I think perforated cardboard is the best way to go, and usually comes included, for free, when you buy the outside packaging. If it's nice cardboard that your product fits really neatly into, customers really appreciate that.

You can also find inserts for your packaging, at office supply stores, VacuForm manufacturers, even your supplier can provide it for you for a fee.

Creating the Ideal Customer Experience

Let's now talk about creating the ideal experience for the customer. If you provide anything extra with your product, it generally enhances your customer's experience and therefore the value of your product. The type of extras I mean are any type of accessories or bonuses that your customer can get with your product.

Customers love accessories, and they love free accessories even more. By identifying compatible accessories, sourcing them cheaply and adding them to your product, it will allow you to not only increase the value of the product, but give you the option to increase the price.

The best place to identify the kind of accessories people want are your competitor's reviews. By going through all of your competitor's reviews (especially the 3 star reviews and below), you will get an idea of the kind of extras people are looking for. It could be a shoulder strap, a carrying case, or an extra set of headphones, etc. By adding it to your product, you enhance the value, and make yourself stand out from your competition.

Bonuses also create a better experience for your customers. By adding a free E-book download with the purchase of your product, it may be what pushes your risk averse customer into finally making the decision to buy. You can deliver that bonus in the form of a little card that you put in with your product packaging. The card will direct them to your website, where they download their free E-book and join your email list.

Replacement parts also work, because sometimes people lose parts quickly. Ask your supplier to see if they can give you extra replacement parts and give them to your customers as bonuses.

These all will help you not only create a great experience for your customers, but also, by adding those things that your competitors are missing, it will help you stand out and become a bestseller very quickly.

CHAPTER 5

Finding High Quality Product Sources

Let's now talk about finding high quality product sources. I mention high quality because there are a lot of wholesalers out there who will sell you all kinds of junk. But we want to focus on the highest quality products. Why? Because we want to help our customers be satisfied. And there's nothing that satisfies customers more than having high quality products that meet their needs, that last, and that they can brag to their friends about.

Also, you want to be proud of the things that you're selling. You want to look forward to selling your product to customers and feel like you can stand behind your product. So again, it is critical to only sell the highest quality products, and that means finding high quality product sources.

But where do you go to find wholesale sources for high quality products? Well, in this chapter we are going to learn:

1. **How to find high quality product suppliers in China and communicate effectively with them.**

   Since you will be working with wholesale sources overseas, you will be speaking with people of a different language, who think differently than you do. And, since we want to make sure that the products that we're getting are of the highest quality possible, communication cannot be left to chance.

2. **How to sample and test our products.**

   You want to make sure to test your product so that you know what you are going to be selling to your customer. And this happens before you put your product in the marketplace.

3. **Negotiating prices and terms with suppliers.**

   Once you've found the product that you want to sell, you then need to negotiate the best price and terms to help you get the healthiest profit. The good news is that wholesale suppliers are generally very flexible, and very willing to negotiate to help you find the right price point. They are looking for a long-term partner, so they will work with you to find a win-win situation.

Finding High Quality Product Sources

So, where do you go to find high quality wholesale product sources? Well, the good news is that in our modern world the Internet has made it very easy for us. There are two very powerful search engines created for finding wholesale sources in China that I am going to talk about, and which we will focus on in this book. One of them is AliExpress, which is the Amazon of China. The other one is Alibaba, which is the behemoth of all wholesale service providers in China and the world.

Now, of course, there are many more product suppliers in the US and many other countries. But I want to focus on these two, specifically, because they're the most user-friendly, they're the ones most used by Americans to source products overseas, and these are the ones that I have successfully used. I want to share with you what works for me so that you can start immediately making multiple streams of income sourcing and selling products on Amazon.

Alibaba

Alibaba.com is China's and the world's biggest online commerce company. Its main sites Taobao, Tmall, Aliexpress and Alibaba.com have hundreds of millions of users, and host millions of merchants and businesses. Alibaba handles more business than any other e-commerce company. Alibaba is also the most popular destination for online shopping, in the world's fastest growing e-commerce market. Transactions on its online sites totaled $248 billion in 2013, more than those of eBay and Amazon combined.

It hosts the greatest list of wholesale suppliers where you can source an abundance of products to sell on Amazon. Alibaba's user-friendly website, makes it easy to find suppliers because it allows you to filter out suppliers according to your criteria. Alibaba also filters out suppliers based on their own quality standards, which more guarantees that you will find a quality supplier for your product.

AliExpress

AliExpress.com is the retail division of Alibaba, and is focused on small volume orders of "ready-made" products designed for the medium and small importers who can't afford to buy a large container of goods.

Since most of the same suppliers from Alibaba are the sellers of retail items on Aliexpress, you can still obtain wholesale pricing for "made to order" products, by contacting sellers on Aliexpress directly and asking them for wholesale pricing.

But why go to AliExpress when you are dealing with the same wholesalers as Alibaba? The reason I go to AliExpress is that you get good feedback information from customers that have previously purchased retail items from these suppliers. This gives you even more data as to the quality of the supplier's products.

Sourcing Products Effectively

The process for sourcing products on Alibaba and AliExpress, is a very straight forward one. It starts by asking the right sourcing questions. Here are the questions I generally email suppliers when I am inquiring about their product:

1. What is the price per piece for bulk orders?
2. Do you have the product available?

3. How long will it take to have it ready to ship?

4. What is the minimum order quantity?

5. What is the shipping cost for the minimum amount?

6. What are your pricing tiers and quantity discounts?

7. Can you send me the label or package design template?

8. Can you add our logo to the unit?

9. What is the price and shipping cost for a sample?

Here is a breakdown to explain the purpose of each question:

1. **What is the price per piece for bulk orders?**—I ask this question because sometimes they don't exactly tell you the price for bulk orders, or the price that is listed on the website is outdated.

2. **Do you have the product available?** Sometimes they may not have the product readily available in stock. They may have to manufacture it. It might even take up to 14 to 45 days to produce. You need to know this so you can understand your timeframe.

3. **How long will it take to have it ready to ship?**—Again, you want to know exactly how much time it will take the product to reach you so you can get your products to your customers.

4. **What is the minimum order quantity (MOQ)?** For many suppliers, they don't want to do business with you unless they know you're going to buy a certain amount. You want to make sure that you have enough capital to buy the minimum amount quantity set by suppliers. The good news is that suppliers are

generally flexible about the minimum order quantity if they know you will buy from them consistently over a long time.

5. **What is the shipping cost for the minimum order quantity?** When they ship you the minimum order quantity, you want to make sure you know exactly how much it costs to ship from overseas. Also, you need this so you can calculate what your exact expense will be, which allows to project the exact return on investment you will have for every sale you make.

   Shipping from overseas will be a lot more expensive than in the United States so be ready to spend more for it. The good news is that when you calculate the shipping cost per piece it doesn't greatly affect your ROI very much.

6. **What are your price tiers and quantity discounts?** Sometimes if you buy more they'll give you more discounts. Get this information up front so you can later plan your inventory in such a way that you can get more discounts.

7. **Can you send me the label or package design template?** Why do I want this? Because I can take the supplier's design template and add my logo to it. Then I can have the supplier print my packaging for me at no extra cost. So you can take the design template, ask a graphic designer on Fiverr.com to add your logo to it and send it back to your supplier to print.

8. **Can you add my logo to your unit (a.k.a.: OEM)?** I want my logo to not just to be on the packaging, I like it to actually be on the actual product itself. This way people can know that it's our product. Granted, you can get away with a product without a

logo and just have your logo on the packaging. But if you want to build a brand, it has more value when people can actually see your logo every time they pick up the product.

9. **What is the price and shipping cost for a sample?** We need to sample the product before we buy from the supplier. We also need samples to test and validate the product on Amazon. You want to know your cost for samples and shipping so you can add this to your budget. Expect the shipping cost to be high for one sample, so you may want to order five to ten samples at a time. This allows you to thoroughly sample the product and to have product that you can test right away on Amazon.

Product Specifications

We want to make sure that we have the accurate specifications or "specs" for the products that we want to buy from the supplier. Product specifications is a big area where a lot of miscommunication can occur and a lot of money lost.

So the easiest way to gather your product specifications is to go to the supplier's description on Alibaba or AliExpress and review the specifications in detail. Once you are satisfied that the specs are correct. You copy and paste those specs in your order to the supplier for your samples. If you need to ask for changes to the specs, the good news is that suppliers are very flexible in making any adjustments to the specifications at your request. They may not be able to make all of the changes, but they can make some. So go ahead and ask.

Another way to get accurate product specifications is to go to your competitors. Go to your competitor's Amazon page, find out what specifications they have for their product, do a little research to make sure they are accurate, make any changes you need, then send these to your supplier.

Sampling and Testing

Now, we talked previously about sampling and testing. This is by far one of the most important parts of wholesale sourcing. Though it is tempting to avoid this step, I tell you from personal experience, that if you try to sell a product that you have not thoroughly sampled and tested, you are in for a world of trouble.

I actually started selling a product that I didn't fully sample and test, and I immediately started receiving complaints from customers because it was a really bad product. That was my own mistake, trying to rush things, and trying to get it out into the marketplace as fast as possible. I swore never to do that again. Now, I only market the product after I've thoroughly tested every sample.

So when you test your samples, test as if you were a consumer. Use your critical eye. Look at it like you just spent $10, $50 or $200 on this product. Look at it in this way because that is what your customers are going to be doing. Make sure you test for quality, durability, user-friendliness, and aesthetics. Ask others to test the samples and give you honest feedback too.

And if you feel any reservations during the testing period, it is a red flag to not sell that product. As a matter of fact, do not sell that product until you feel completely confident that the product is of the highest of quality.

Try to get samples sent to you at a discount, or with free shipping. I wouldn't suggest getting free samples, because you will probably receive a customer return or a sample that is not like the future product you will order. Sometimes you have to pay full price, but it's well worth it. And If the sample doesn't meet your criteria, you can always sell it on EBay and recoup some of your money back.

Negotiating Rates and Terms

Once you approve the samples it's time to negotiate the best rates and the quantities you need from your supplier. Although suppliers put their prices and minimum order quantities on the Alibaba or AliExpress website, they are not fixed in stone. Suppliers are generally very flexible because they want to establish a long-term business relationship with you.

Your goal is to get the best price possible, without reducing the quality of your product. Personally, I don't mind paying the highest price for a high quality product because I know I can sell it for three, four, or even five times as much and make a great profit from it. Even though I spend a little bit more, it doesn't matter, because my customer is happy, the supplier is happy and I'm happy. So don't be cheap.

One way to negotiate a better price is to order a higher amount of products, and ask for a discount. Another way is to search around for your supplier's competitors to find better pricing, and use this information as a basis for bargaining for a better price from the supplier you want to do business with. Last, you can convince your supplier to give you better pricing by establishing a paying relationship with them for a period of time, and asking them later to drop pricing because of your good paying history.

Using Alibaba to Find Great Products— The System

Here is the process I use when searching for the best wholesale suppliers on Alibaba.com:

1. On the Alibaba search bar, click on Advanced Search.

2. Copy and paste the title of the product from the Amazon Bestseller list and put in the Search bar (max 50 characters).

3. Tick the Gold Supplier button, then click search.

4. When search results appear, tick the button on top that says "On Site Check."

5. *(Optional)*—Tick the button on top that says "Assessed Supplier."

6. Click on the "Contact Supplier" button to send an email to the supplier.

7. Cut and paste the "Sourcing Questions" in your email, so that you get as much information as you can from the supplier. Here are the sourcing questions I use in Alibaba:

   - What is the price per piece for bulk orders?

   - Do you have the product available?

   - How long will it take to have it ready to ship?

   - What is the minimum order quantity?

   - What is the shipping cost for the minimum amount?

   - What are your pricing tiers and quantity discounts?

   - Can you send me the label or package design template?

- Can you add our logo to the unit?

- What is the price and shipping cost for a sample?

8. Wait for the supplier to get back to you with their answers.

Using AliExpress to Find Great Products— The System

AliExpress.com is primarily focused on selling at retail prices. But since the sellers on AliExpress get the bulk of their business through wholesale supply relationships (actually their retail sales account for only 10% of their revenue), they are more interested in giving you wholesale pricing. If you contact the supplier directly and ask for wholesale pricing and terms, they will jump at the chance to work with you. Here is the process that I use:

1. Copy the title of the product from the Amazon Bestseller List and put it in the search bar on AliExpress (max 50 characters).

2. Go through the list of product results, and click on the product you are looking for.

3. Click on the "Contact Supplier" button to send an email to the supplier.

4. Cut and paste the "Sourcing Questions" so that you get as much information as you can from the supplier. Here are the sourcing questions I usually ask in AliExpress:

- What is the price per piece for bulk orders?

- Do you have the product available?

- How long will it take to have it ready to ship?
- What is the minimum order quantity?
- What is the shipping cost for the minimum amount?
- What are your pricing tiers and quantity discounts?
- Can you send me the label or package design template?
- Can you add our logo to the unit?
- What is the price and shipping cost for a sample? (Since AliExpress already has sample and shipping information I usually skip this question).

5. Wait for the supplier to get back to you with their answers.

CHAPTER 6

Getting the Most Profit for Your Amazon Sales

Now let's talk about creating the highest profit situation from your Amazon Sales. When you sell on Amazon, you want to make sure that you make the highest possible profit while spending the least amount of money.

The big question is, "How are you able to manage the expenses and charge the right prices so you can get the highest profit situation?" Generally, it will take two things:

1. Establishing the best pricing for your product, and

2. Minimizing expense without losing product quality.

Choosing the Best Price for Your Product

Generally, you have two options when it comes to pricing. You can price your product based on what everybody else is pricing, or, even better, you can create enough value with your unique brand that you can charge the highest prices.

This is especially true on Amazon. People go to Amazon to spend more money. They do not mind spending extra money on products because they know that it's coming from Amazon; and they know they will have a great experience. Because of this, on Amazon, if you create a valuable and unique brand with a lot of benefits, your customers will be willing to pay a lot more.

So, from a practical standpoint, a good goal for your pricing is to aim for getting an 100 percent return on investment, or more, after all your expenses. This is actually very common when you're dealing with your own products (also known as private label products). People who create their own brand, have more control on what they spend for expenses, and they are able to create massive value with their brand that results in getting double the amount of profit.

For a great Amazon Profit/ Cost Calculator to calculate your Amazon product ROI go to **Amazonsellingsecretsbook.com/cost-calculator** to download.

Pricing for Success

There are two main approaches for pricing in Amazon that will give you the most control over how much profit and sales you make. They are:

1. **Pricing for Value**—This involves charging high prices to capture the market of high value customers. In other words, charge the highest prices in your industry or in your product category to attract the customers that are willing to pay the highest prices.

2. **Pricing for Momentum**—This is when you price low in order to get a high sales volume and to build the sales momentum that you need. After you have achieved the sales volume you want (usually to get on the Bestseller list) you incrementally raise prices to your ideal level.

Pricing for Value

Pricing has the power to create high value in the mind of a customer. Have you ever had the experience, that when you saw the high price of a product, all of a sudden you considered that product to be of high value? In other words, your mind was automatically influenced to believe it was a high value product because the price was so high. This is the influence that comes with pricing at higher levels.

Pricing for Value comes with certain benefits and challenges. As for benefits, 1) you get higher profits for each product you sell; 2) you attract higher quality customers; and 3) your higher quality customers tend to refer other higher quality customers, who have money to spend on your product.

Another benefit of pricing for value is that the higher you price your products, the greater value your brand will have. Customers will associate your high value products with your brand and will automatically see your brand as a high value brand in the future.

Pricing for Value also has its challenges. Higher pricing takes more time to build sales momentum because there's not a lot of people out there who have the means to buy higher priced products. Also, a big chunk of the people who go to Amazon go to find deals, so price sensitive customers will avoid your product. Last, in general, there are a smaller amount of customers who are willing to pay high prices for products in any marketplace.

How to Successfully Price for Value

If you are going to price for value, here is a strategy that has been successful for many value pricing Amazon Sellers:

1. Find out what the highest price is for similar products in your category.

2. Either price higher than your higher priced competitors or price equal to them.

3. Get a lot of social proof through abundant reviews. This is critical since higher value customers tend to rely on the experience of others to make their buying choices.

4. Lower your price incrementally every day, until people start buying your product at your ideal profit goal. Lowering your price by $5 a day should give you good results.

Pricing for Momentum

Pricing for Momentum means to price as low as possible in the beginning in order to immediately start making sales. After you generate enough sales momentum, then you increase the price until you identify the ideal target price that will bring you the most daily sales and most profit.

This is by far the most successful strategy in pricing in the Amazon Marketplace. It is successful because it is based on the principle that customers have an ideal target price where a multitude of them will buy. The ideal target price is the price that gives you the ideal profit you need, and motivates the most customers possible to purchase your product because it makes sense to them.

Promotions are the key to pricing for momentum. When I say promotional pricing I mean lowering your prices so that people feel like they're getting a great deal, when they compare the value they are getting for the price. By reducing your prices temporarily, it will get a flurry of people buying your product. This will increase your sales rank which will also give you more exposure and more sales. Then you can begin to incrementally raise prices until you reach your ideal target price. For the best results, its best to run these promotions on weekends, where the most people are on Amazon looking for something to spend their money on.

What are the benefits of promotional pricing? 1) More sales. That's the immediate and greatest benefit. 2) A lot more people will buy your product. 3) More consistent sales. Why? Because all of the extra sales will mean that Amazon will promote you more, which means more people will find your product. 4) More volume means more reviews, so you can have more people give you reviews, which also improves your sales rank. 5) More sales volume means reaching the Amazon Bestseller list, which leads to more exposure to more buying customers.

Now, what are the challenges to promotional pricing? Profits are lower. You're going to have to do a whole lot more volume to be able to get the profits you are looking for. Also, volume sales means more returns, so though a lot more people are going to buy, a lot more will also be returning.

Also with lower prices, you tend to attract more price sensitive customers. Price customers, tend to be more demanding, they tend to complain more, and they'll end up returning your product and giving you a negative review. So if you price on the lower end, you tend to attract more of these people and there is not much you can do about it. So, sometimes you have to be careful if you're going to be on the lower end of the price spectrum.

Another challenge of promotional pricing is that if you go too low it may affect the value of your brand. Once you drop below a certain threshold, people will perceive the lower price as lower value, and associate it with your brand. So you will end up cheapening your brand by pricing too low.

Last, promotional pricing tends to have a lot more competition because 80 percent of the time lowering prices tends to be the market strategy for most sellers on Amazon. Many do not know they're shooting themselves in the foot, but that's the general way that most people approach selling on Amazon. This automatically means you're going to have a lot more competition. More competition also creates the potential for a "race to the bottom" situation where you just keep undercutting each other's prices until you're not really making much of a profit.

How to Successfully Price for Momentum

Here is the best way to succeed if you decide to use the Price for Momentum Strategy:

1. Set your price as low as you can, but make sure you are still making a profit. Or look at your competitor's pricing and either match it, or go a bit lower.

2. When you start getting sales, incrementally raise the price every day. Raising your price by $5 a day should give you good results.

3. When you get great ranking on the bestseller list (Spots numbers 1—6), begin to incrementally raise your prices. Note: If you hit #1 in the bestseller list for your category, you may want to consider keeping it at the #1 bestseller price. The volume may justify the lower profit. Also, see if you could raise the price and still stay at the #1 Bestseller spot.

4. If you raise price and start seeing sales slowdown, lower your prices to its previous level.

5. Don't forget to get reviews. Reviews will help you to motivate more customers to buy, because it adds more value to your product.

Consider running weekly or monthly promotions to kick-start the momentum again in case it starts slowing down or to just to keep up the momentum. Weekends and evenings are great because that's when people are at home and that's when they make a lot of purchases. The second or third week of the month tends to be good for promotions too, because this is after customers have paid all their bills and they have some extra time and money to spend.

CHAPTER 7

Creating a High Converting Listing

Creating a high converting Amazon listing is one of the most crucial steps in successfully selling on Amazon. Why? Because this is your advertising page. This is the page that people are going to come to and determine whether they see enough value in your product to pull out their wallet and buy from you.

So how does one create a high converting listing? High converting listings are created using a few key components, including:

1. Creating the best converting title for your product.

2. Adding emotionally compelling images that will motivate people to buy.

3. Writing high converting bullets and descriptions that motivate people to purchase your product.

4. Providing valuable bonuses to motivate customers to make the decision to buy from you.

Creating a High Converting Title

The title is the main description of your product. There are few criteria that makes a really high converting product title. And the great thing about Amazon is that it gives you a lot of room to add a whole lot of other words to really beef up you title. Here are a few elements that make for a high converting title:

1. **Your Brand**—You want the brand name in your title, because eventually your brand is going to become popular enough that people actually look for you.

2. **Your Product Name**—Put your product's unique name in the title, next to your brand, so that you can create immediate value in the mind of your customer. For example, if you are selling baking products, you would put your brand, "Baker's Delight," next to your product's unique name, " Fascinating Cupcake Liners," at the start of your title.

3. **Product Description**—People want to make sure they know what they're buying, so make sure you let them know, that they are in the right place by giving a clear description of what you are selling.

4. **Your USP**—You want to add your USP in the title because it is the one thing that makes you stand out from your competition, and the unique selling proposition that tells your customers that your product is better or different from everyone else's.

   Personally, I like to put the USP in all caps so that people will not miss it.

5. **Product Benefits**—You want to add the greatest benefits your product brings so that customer will be immediately motivated to either buy your product, or read more of your listing. Going with our previous example, your title will end up looking like this (this is an actual product that is currently the Amazon Bestseller in its category and an example of a great title; I've just changed the brand name):

> "Baker's Delight Fascinating Silicone Baking Cups—Set of 12 Reusable Cupcake Liners in Six Vibrant Colors in Storage Container—Muffin, Gelatin, Snacks, Frozen Treats, Ice Cream or Chocolate Shell-lined Dessert Molds—Great for Bento Lunch Boxes—BPA Free Food Grade Silicone Non-stick Bake ware— VIBRANT SILICONE BAKING CUPS."

Look at all of the benefits it conveys—Reusable, Vibrant colors, Great for Bento Lunch Boxes, Non-stick—BPA Free, etc.

Now some people will tell you not to add so much in the title. But after continual testing, it is pretty obvious that the more benefits you add to the title, the more people will buy. This is because the benefits motivates the person to continue to read my description and think, "Wow! This product has everything I've been looking for." That's the response I want people to have, so I'll add as many benefits as Amazon will allow in the title.

6. **Keywords**—I also list keywords in the title. Why? Because search engines do find those Amazon pages as well. So I will use a keyword tool to identify the most popular keywords for my product both in the search engines and in Amazon.

Google Keyword Planner or FreshKey are good services you can use to find the most popular product words.

When using keywords, you also have to make sure that it fits well with your product title, so that it can both motivate customers to buy, but also be easily found by search engines. In other words, string it together in such a way that people feel like it just flows well.

One thing that you will find is that your initial title may not be the one that converts. So you have to keep testing it. Just keep making tweaks every day or every couple days, until you find the right listing that will get people to start pulling out their wallets.

Use Emotionally Compelling Images

Another critical area to success of your Amazon listing, is the use of emotionally compelling Amazon images. Every Amazon listing is required to have a picture; and if you don't have one, it keeps your product from being listed in their general product category listing.

But if you want to create a high converting listing, it's not enough just to have a picture. You have to make sure you have an emotionally compelling picture that motivates people to buy. Also, one picture is not enough. If you want people to buy, you need to fill it up with six to eight high quality pictures.

Another important key to motivating customers through your images, is to make your images a minimum of 1,000 by 1,000 pixels. This is because there's something about the zoom feature (when you hover over the picture and it just pops out) that customers love and that motivates them to buy.

How do you choose an emotionally compelling image to use? You want to make sure you get images that show a lot of the benefits that people are going to get from buying the product. You want the kind of images that give them a glimpse of how happy they will be from using the product. In other words, what the product is going to do for them, the product in action, and the product in the best light possible.

Turning pictures into emotionally compelling images is a lot easier than you think. You can find product images by either asking your supplier, or buying stock photo. Then you can go to Fiverr.com or Elance.com and hire a graphic designer to tweak the pictures for you. They can add your product, brand or logo to the picture and adjust the picture to convey any message you want. That is the magic of Photoshop.

You can also get picture ideas from your competitors. You can find stock photo that is similar to your competitor's pictures, and edit them enough so that they become new pictures with your product and logo. I am not saying take competitor's product pictures and add them to your listing; remember we want to be unique, and that is just unethical. Rather, borrow their picture ideas, get similar stock photo, and edit it until it is original and conveys the message you want to give your customers.

Remember, you need six to eight high quality pictures, so don't settle for one or two. Get as many as you can. And the more pictures your customer has to look at, the more convinced they'll be to buy. Amazon does not allow you to add text to your pictures, so it is up to your images themselves to communicate the best message possible.

Product Bullets and Descriptions

The Product Description is a combination between the bulleted description and the main product description. The bulleted description are the bulleted list of information that are under the product title and to the right of the image. The main description is the main area toward the middle of the page under the title "Product Description."

In order to create high converting bullet points, I generally focus on just making sure you add as many benefits as you can. I also put the title of the bullet in all caps and the details in regular letters. This way it can really stand out for people who don't like to read the details. You also want to list the bullets in order of priority: the most valuable benefit first, then the next most valuable benefit, and so on. Also, for each bullet put as much information as possible and use up all of the character space Amazon gives you. The more detail the better, especially for customers that need to read the details to make a buying decision.

Here is an example of the bullets from the Cupcake Liner Listing:

- REUSABLE—Set of 12 reusable silicone baking cups in six fun, vibrant colors (pink, orange, yellow, green, blue and purple) in a convenient storage container. Makes lunchtime fun as colorful dividers for bento lunch boxes.

- PREMIUM QUALITY—Our silicone baking cups are of premium quality and are thicker than the competition provide worry-free use and hold up better over time. Each cup measures 2-5/8-inch dia x 1.25-inch tall and holds 2-1/4 fluid ounces to the rim.

- BPA FREE—Our technology ensures optimum baking performance, and our highest quality, advanced BPA-Free, FDA approved food grade silicone non-stick bakeware safeguards your health and resists stains. Versatile silicone molds have so many different uses, and are a blast for all ages!

- MULTIPLE USES—Great for cupcakes, muffins, cheesecakes, chocolate bowls, gelatin, frozen snacks and desserts, cooking eggs and other dishes. No muffin pan is necessary—just place baking cups directly on cooking sheet, place on middle oven rack and bake. Heat resistant to 475 F, freezer, microwave and top-rack dishwasher safe.

- LIFETIME REPLACEMENT GUARANTEE—We guarantee that we will replace your item at any point during the life of the product.

For the main product description in the middle of the page, I like to focus on the five P's. Now, the five P's are designed to focus on the five things that will help motivate the customer most to buy your product. The five P's include:

1. **The Problem**—Talk about their problem. Talk about the problem that your product fixes. Why? Because that is why they're coming to look at your product, They have an issue or conflict or something that they needs fixing and they think your product can do it for them. Also, as soon as you touch upon their problem, they feel like you understand them and they feel like they want to hear more of what you have to say.

2. **The Promise**—Tell them what your product can do. List all of the benefits that your product promises and how it can alleviate all their pain, help them be happier, help them be healthier, sexier, leaner, thinner, richer, whatever it is. Go ahead and start giving them all those promises.

   Now you don't want to sell it too much because people don't like to be sold, they like to buy. But they do appreciate people who help them to buy. So make the promise in such a way that helps them see all of the benefits they will be getting by buying your product.

3. **The Picture**—Besides your product pictures, this is your opportunity to create mental pictures for them. Start describing what a vision of a better future using your product will look like. Describe it in visual words. Give them a story, give them an idea in their heads. Your actual pictures will help, but by describing it further to them it motivates them even more.

4. **The Proof**—Add supporting evidence that your product can fulfill on its promise, whether in the form of credentials, statistics, studies, and certifications. These will help the customer make a better decision because they feel like they are reducing their risk.

   Note: As of the writing of this book, Amazon does not allow testimonials in the product description; so stick to credentials, studies and certifications if you have them.

5. **The Push**—Make sure you encourage your customers to buy, by putting on the bottom of the description the direct suggestion to, "Buy Now!" or "Get yours today!"

Many Amazon listings do not have this kind of call to action, and I don't understand why. But you need to put it in there and make it very commanding, so people can take action on all your suggestions.

Adding Valuable Bonuses

You may think that the title, images and description is enough to get a customer to buy. 80% of the time you would be right. But, people need as much reason to buy as possible, because price is usually an issue. So, if you can create enough value to outweigh the risk in buying, you will always have a sale.

So, add a lot of valuable bonuses. Give away many free bonuses that will make your product more valuable in the eyes of your customer. This includes valuable accessories. If you can add an accessory, throw it in there. It could be a case, it could be a wrist strap, it could be extra batteries, etc. If it is valuable in the eyes of your customer, add it in and your product will become even more valuable.

I like offering a free EBook download in my listing. They can get access to it through a postcard that I add in the product packaging. The postcard then sends the customer to a website to download their free eBooks. The benefit of this is that I can capture their contact information and add them on my email list for future promotions.

You can get great eBooks from private label rights websites that sell eBooks that deal with your specific subject. They sell them for anywhere from $1.00—$6.00, but once you buy it, you now have the rights to give it away to your customers as a free download as many times as you want.

Another bonus you can offer is to add a competitor product as a complimentary item for free. If there's something that your competitor is selling that would greatly compliment your product as an accessory, go ahead and bundle them together and sell the product at the same or higher price. This will motivate your customer to buy because they see all the powerful value that they're getting from your product bundle.

Listing Your First Amazon Product

You've got to get familiar with how to list your products on Amazon so that you can use your listing to its fullest potential. Amazon Seller Central provides you with general training on how to do this. I have also provided you a simple process you can use to get your first product set up to sell on Amazon. Here are the steps you will take when listing your product in Amazon's catalog:

1. In your Amazon Seller Central account, hover over the "Inventory" tab on the top of the page and click on "Add a Product."

2. Click on Create a New Product. Because you are creating a new product with your brand, it doesn't exist in the Amazon catalog, so you need to list it as new.

3. Fill out the product listing form, focusing on the following specific areas:

4. Product Category—choose the correct category and subcategory for your product.

5. Product Title—Add the main title for your product.

6. Brand—Add the brand name for your product line.

7. Manufacturer—Since it is your product, you can register your brand in Amazon as the manufacturer.

8. Manufacturer Part Number—Assign an alphanumeric code for your product.

9. UPC code—You can purchase these online from a reputable UPC seller or you can purchase them inexpensively from EBay. You need a UPC code to list your product.

10. Condition—For the product's condition, choose "New" from the drop down menu.

11. Product Price—Add the price you will offer for your product.

12. Sale Price—(optional) In case you are running a promotion, add the sale price and the date range the promotion will run.

13. Shipping Method—If your product is in testing phase, then choose yourself (merchant) for shipping method. If you intend to have Amazon ship for you, then choose the button giving Amazon the shipping responsibility (FBA).

14. Quantity—If you choose to ship yourself, you need to then go back to the form and add the quantity of units you have on hand.

15. Product Images—Upload 6—8 great images you can use to display your product. Make sure they are a minimum of 1000X1000 pixels.

16. Product Description—Add the product's bulleted description and main description.

17. Product Keywords—Add the best product keywords, so that people can find your product when they do a search.

18. Save—Click on the save button and your product will be listed in Amazon in the next 15 minutes.

19. Review—Review your listing to make sure everything turned out the way you want it to.

CHAPTER
8

Testing and Validation

The main purpose of testing and validation is to see if people even want your product. You can come up with the best product in the world, and find a great source for it; but if nobody wants your product, it's going to be a waste of your time and money.

This happens a lot to new Amazon Sellers. They believe that because they love their own product, then everyone else is going to want their product also. Ultimately, when they finally list their product, the reality hits when they realize they are not getting any sales.

On the contrary, the only way to truly know if your product will be successful is to test it in the marketplace. Only if you throw your product in the marketplace and people buy it with cold, hard cash, will you know if it will be successful.

Another purpose of testing is to get accustomed to the entire Amazon selling process from sourcing to selling. When you first start out there is a steep learning curve, but the more you get accustomed to the process of sourcing and selling on Amazon, the easier it becomes and the more efficient you become. You learn how to avoid problems with your supplier, you set up better systems for receiving your product, and you distribute your products more efficiently on Amazon. Next thing you know, you're making a lot of money selling your products with very little effort.

Testing and validation is also essential to verify how effective your Amazon listing is. The more you tweak and test your listing, and the more buyer response you get, the closer you will be to finding the ideal listing that compels most customers to buy.

Pricing also benefits greatly from testing. The more you test different pricing levels, the closer you get to the ideal target price which will bring you the most customers and the most profit.

Testing also helps us identify any problems, issues, and bottlenecks in the entire process that you follow. In other words, testing helps you identify if there are things that are going to prevent you from having a streamlined process of getting your products out to customers, and keeping them happy. Testing also helps you get good feedback so you can confirm what is satisfying your customers and what is not. We cannot just assume that our customers will respond the way we want them to, or that they will value every feature of our products. When you are testing, the feedback you receive from customers helps to clarify what your customers are really thinking.

How to Test and Validate Your Products

This is the process that I follow to test products in the marketplace, that has been very effective for me:

1. **Initially, order five samples from your supplier to test for quality.** This includes testing the samples to make sure that the product is high quality, durable, user-friendly, and that it is aesthetically pleasing (that it looks good). The reason I choose five samples is that sometimes the samples they send you are not the same as the products you will order in the future. By ordering five, I get a good idea of the product I will be working with. Also, I can verify if the quality is consistent with all of the samples.

   This also allows you to test the process of working with your supplier. When you order and receive your samples, here are a few questions you can ask yourself: 1) Did they send the package in a safe, protected package that will prevent breakage? 2) Do they take a safe form of payment like PayPal? 3) What shipping company did they use and can you trust the shipping company?

   On a side note, in regards to shipping, your best bet is to stick with American carriers like FEDEX, UPS and DHL. Stay away from the Chinese Delivery company called EMS. If something goes wrong with your package, you won't be able to speak with an English speaking person to resolve the issue.

2. **After you test your samples, order another 10–20 units to test on Amazon.** Once you confirm that the product is of high quality, then you need to test it in the marketplace. The idea is that if you can sell 10 units in a month, then there is a good chance

that more people will want to buy your product. If you can't sell 10 units in a month, even after extensive testing, then that is confirmation that people will probably not want to buy your product.

You can usually get the supplier to give you wholesale pricing for the 10—20 units by telling them that you are buying them for testing purposes. It also makes more sense to buy 10—20 to justify the large shipping cost.

3. **List the product on Amazon.** Use all of the different criteria we listed in previous chapters (title, images, description, and bonuses) and list the product. Since you are only testing, you don't have to go through all the process of expertly "Photoshopping" images like I mentioned previously. At this point, the suppliers pictures will work just fine.

   Test your titles by adding different benefits. Keep swapping out benefits in your title to see which one most resonates with people. Test the product name, too. Test your images by rotating images, or swapping out images to see which works best. Test your descriptions and bullet points by changing the five P's (The problem, the promise, the picture, the proof, the push). Test your bonuses. Try one downloadable book, or give them another one. Try one accessory, and if that doesn't work, try another accessory. Keep tweaking and testing, little by little, every day, until you find the listing that really resonates with customers (meaning that it will drive customers to buy).

4. **Test Your Pricing**—Choose whether you are going to price for momentum or price for value. Pricing for momentum

includes pricing your product at a comparable or lower price to your competitors. Incrementally raise prices until the sales slowdown. Then go back to the previous level you were at that produced daily sales.

Pricing for value means pricing it at a high price, and then lower your price incrementally until customers begin to buy daily.

5. **Packaging and Shipping**—Choose your preliminary packaging to fulfill and test orders. Now, it won't be the fancy packaging with your logo on it, but choose something that's nice. Then test the process of getting the orders, packaging the orders, sending out the orders to your customers and making sure your customers are happy. Prepare the inserts you will put in your packaging; whether product materials, free bonuses, product instructions, etc.

When you test your packaging and shipping in this way, it shows you how good, or how fast you are in your ability to fulfill on orders.

6. **Feedback and Reviews**—Ask your first couple customers about how they feel about your products. "Did they like your product?" "What didn't they like about your product?" In other words, be very specific in the questions you ask your customers, and they'll be glad to tell you because they want a great product.

If they really liked your product, ask them for reviews. Begin to collect reviews that will help to build your product value and sales rank in Amazon.

Expectations When You're Testing

You can expect it to be about two to three weeks before you actually get your first sale. Sometimes, you can get sales right away (especially if you price for momentum), but don't be discouraged if you don't see a sale for two to three weeks.

Once you do get sales, remember the focus is testing, not on making money. You are only gathering data, so every situation is a learning opportunity. Everything that does not go the way you want it, is an opportunity for you to learn and more streamline your process.

Customers will tend to buy more on certain days than others, buy more on certain times of the day than others; and buy more on certain months than others. Keep testing and gathering information until you have a good understanding of the buying patterns of your customers.

Expect to wait 60 days to have enough data to determine if your product is a winner or a loser. Keep tweaking and testing everything until you start making daily sales, or until you conclude that there is no viable market for the product.

Validating All of Your Data

After you have gathered all of this information, how can you tell if your product passed the test? Here are the criteria I use to determine if I have a winning product on Amazon:

1. **Sales Validation.** If you can sell 10 products in a month, then you have a product that you can build a business around. If you can't get 10 sales in a month, then forget it. You probably

don't have a product that people are interested in. Now this is good news, because it means you can avoid wasting time, but instead you can go out and look for another product and try it again.

2. **Price Validation**—How do I know if people will continue to buy at a certain price? If I can get two or three sales at a certain price point, within a span of a few days, then I feel confident that I can keep it at that price point and more will buy. One sale at a certain price may be a fluke. Two sales I feel better about. Three, four, five sales means that I got something that's hot, and that I've found the right price point that will work for customers.

3. **Customer Satisfaction Validation**—How do you know if customers are satisfied? If you receive multiple four to five star reviews from verified purchasers, then you know your product is satisfying customers(a verified purchaser is someone who has actually bought your product and gives a review). Since only 10 percent of customers on Amazon give reviews, then you know you're doing something right and the customers are happy with the product.

CHAPTER
9

Order Fulfillment and Inventory Management

In this section of our book I'm going to talk about effective order fulfillment and inventory management. In other words, fulfilling your orders to customers and then making sure you have enough inventory to continue to sell and make money.

In order to effectively manage your inventory it is going to take two things:

1. Effectively getting the product to the customer. Finding the most effective and efficient way to get orders fulfilled in a way that keeps customer's happy.

2. Managing your inventory needs. This includes making sure you always have just enough products to fulfill on all your orders. I say just enough because you don't want too much inventory. Having a lot of inventory that is not making money will not do you any good and only ties up your money.

Getting Your Products to Your Customers

There are three simple principles to effectively get your products to customers in a way that will create highly satisfied customers. This includes:

1. **Provide a quick response.** In other words, as soon as you get the order you want to make sure that the order is being processed and prepared for shipping within one to two days.

2. **Package the product effectively.** You will need an efficient packaging process so that that the product gets to your customer safe and sound. You'll need 1) the product packaging box, whether it's going to be a generic nice looking box, or a specially designed box with your logo and branding. 2) You will need inserts to protect the package which can be either perforated cardboard, VacuForm plastic, crinkle cut filler, etc. 3) Product inserts, whether that's a postcard with instructions for your free bonus, product instructions, product detail sheet, promotions, or a request for reviews. 4) And of course, you need your product—make sure you don't forget that.

3. **Shipping system.** Last, you will need a cost effective shipping system including: 1) Shipping boxes including their size and weight (the shipping carrier will ask for this). 2) Shipping labels that you can either purchase directly through Amazon, or through your carrier; and 3) packing slips, which you can print directly through your Amazon Seller Central Account.

Fulfillment By Amazon

Most of the packing and shipping process discussed is based on doing the shipping yourself. You also have the option of choosing to have Amazon do the shipping for you through a program called Fulfillment by Amazon or FBA.

What is FBA? Fulfillment by Amazon (FBA) is when you opt to have all your inventory stored at one of Amazon's warehouses. Whenever an order is placed by your customers, Amazon will pick, package, then ship your product to the customer, and you don't have to do a thing. In other words, you outsource the entire process of fulfilling your promises to your customers to Amazon. Since Amazon has one of the most successful distribution systems in the world, it is a smart move for most Amazon Sellers.

With FBA, you don't have to carry inventory. The orders are automatically taken care of for you when they are placed by your customers. Amazon handles all of the customer service questions, as well as any returns. Amazon also informs you if your inventory is running low so you can replenish your stock. In essence Amazon handles the entire fulfillment process for you, automating this portion of your Amazon selling business for you.

The cost is reasonable. And if you are used to shipping via priority mail, then using FBA actually saves you money.

If you would like tutorials on how to use FBA, then go to the Amazon FBA website, and they will give you free access to FBA training videos and PDF tutorials to help you manage the process. The training also gives you pricing comparison charts so you can see how much money you're saving if you do the product fulfillment yourself or if you do it through Amazon FBA.

Here's a list of the many benefits you get from using FBA:

1. **FBA automatically enrolls your product in Amazon Prime.** Being part of the group of Prime eligible products means Amazon Prime customers can get your product with free shipping, in 2 days. If you don't know what Prime is, Amazon Prime is a special program that allows members to receive a host of benefits, including free 2 day shipping on any products they order.

   So, if you enroll in FBA, your product becomes Prime eligible, which means shipping is free to the customer and they can get their product sooner. This is good news for you, because it motivates your customers to buy more.

2. **Customers are willing to pay more.** Knowing that your product has the Amazon seal of approval makes customers see more value in your product and motivates them to pay more. Amazon's endorsement gives customers the peace of mind of knowing they will be cared for by Amazon if they ever have an issue. This gives you the flexibility to charge higher prices.

3. **You will get better sales rank.** Amazon ranks you compared to other competitors based on your sales volume, revenue and reviews. If you're competing against another seller who is not FBA, you will benefit by getting better sales ranking, as well has having Amazon promote you more, because you fulfill your orders through Amazon.

Now FBA is not perfect. It does come with a few challenges including:

1. **Expense**—Using FBA can be more expensive than fulfilling orders yourself. It also may not be cost effective, especially if you are selling a low priced product.

2. **Loss of control**—You are passing control of your inventory to Amazon, which gives you less ability to influence what happens with your inventory.

3. **Amazon may lose your inventory**—Sometimes, Amazon may lose your inventory and there is little you can do about it. You can get reimbursed for the loss, but at a rate that Amazon determines.

4. **Sales tax issues**—Amazon stores your inventory in multiple warehouses in different states in order to quickly fulfill on orders. Generally, states will tax you based on where you keep your inventory, so by using FBA you will have to file and pay sales tax in multiple states. A solution for this is to pay to use Amazon's FBA Inventory Placement option, and have all of your inventory stored in one warehouse. Yet it is up to Amazon to pick the warehouse, which may or may not fit your needs.

Effectively Managing Your Inventory

Effective inventory management is essential because if you identify a high selling product that is making you a lot of money, you don't want to run out of inventory. But rather you want to keep selling till the cows come home. On the other hand, you don't want to have too much inventory either, because you will just end up tying up your cash until your inventory sells.

The best way to manage your inventory is through establishing an inventory management calendar that can project and organize your inventory needs for an entire year.

An effective inventory management calendar has a few important components. These include:

1. **Average Daily Sales Number.** When you know how many sales you make daily, this gives you a good idea as to how many units you will need per month. Since it is an average, you will be ordering a few more to account for big sale days.

2. **Monthly Stock Need.** This is the average daily sales number multiplied times the number of days in the month. For example, if you sell 20 units a day, then your monthly stock need will be 600 units (20units/day X 30 days = 600 units).

3. **Stock Lead Time.** This is the amount of time it takes for your supplier to get your stock to you. If you use FBA, this also includes the amount of time that it takes you to get your inventory to the Amazon FBA warehouse.

4. **Months and Holidays.** When you are selling on Amazon, each month is not created equal. Some months will have higher

sales volume than others, while other months will have higher returns than others. Knowing all of the months and major holidays will prepare you to order more or less depending on the need for the month.

5. **Budget.** All this information means little unless you have the money or credit to buy your product from the supplier. You need to project your inventory needs, the amount of money you will need, and when you need it, to make sure you can purchase the inventory when necessary.

Using Your Inventory Management Calendar Effectively

An Inventory Management Calendar can streamline your entire inventory process if used effectively. Therefore, it is essential to know how to utilize it to its fullest potential. This is the process that I use, that works most effectively for me:

1. Identify your average daily sales number.

2. Identify all of the retail holidays in the calendar year.

3. Identify your monthly stock needs based on the particular month. Usually you can count on the following inventory criteria to help prepare you to have enough inventory for regular months and holidays:

   • *Regular month:* Total Monthly Inventory Need = Average daily sales X number of days in month.

- *Retail holiday month:* Total Monthly Inventory Need X 2

- *November—(Pre-Christmas month):* Total Monthly Inventory Need X 3

- *December (Christmas month):* Total Monthly Inventory Need =X 4

4. Use the Stock Lead Time information to determine when you need to order inventory and mark these dates on your calendar. These are your Inventory Order Dates.

5. Calculate the amount of money you will need by the Inventory Order Dates and plan on getting the cash or credit by that date.

Advanced Inventory Management Tips

Here are a few more tips to help you to more effectively manage your inventory:

1. If you have the capital, order your inventory on a quarterly basis. You can use the same Inventory Management Process, but manage it on a quarterly versus a monthly basis. Consider using a credit card with reward points so you can get cash back.

2. Try to get your supplier to give you 90, 60, or 30 day Net terms (this means they will send you the product and give you 90, 60 or 30 days to pay for it). This way you can order the product first, then pay for it with your sales.

3. If you cannot get Net terms, negotiate "just in time" supplying from your wholesale source. "Just in time," means that your

supplier will produce and stock your inventory at their warehouse at no cost, and will ship it to you when you need it.

4. Make sure you obtain your suppliers holiday schedule so that you know when they are not open. Add this to your Inventory Management Calendar so you can prepare for it. You don't want to be in a situation where you desperately need inventory, and you find out your supplier is closed for a week.

5. Train your supplier to package your product for you. If your supplier is wiling (usually for an extra cost) have them print and assemble your logo packaging and inserts.

6. If you use FBA, train your supplier to package your products and send them to Amazon FBA directly. Make sure you have verified that your supplier can meet your product quality standards before you do this.

Funding Your Inventory

I generally lean more toward preserving cash and using other people's money besides using my own. Especially when I can have my suppliers provide me with credit lines or 90, 60 or 30 Day terms. Remember, every one of your suppliers have the ability to extend Net terms or credit to you as a retailer. This includes your product supplier, accessories supplier, product packaging supplier, product labeling supplier, etc. Even Amazon is capable of extending terms and loans for Amazon sellers.

If you can obtain revolving credit, this is even better than Net 90, 60 or 30 day terms. This is especially useful if you have to buy packaging for your product. Packaging companies want to sell you 1000 pieces of packaging at a time or more, which you are going to use throughout the whole year. If you are going to sell the packaging with your product throughout the whole year, its best to spread the cost over the year through revolving credit. Revolving credit includes personal and business credit cards, supply revolving credit cards, and credit lines as well.

Inventory financing is another option for Amazon sellers to cover cost of high inventory seasons like Christmas. Inventory financing is when someone lends you the money to buy your inventory, for pre-determined interest amount, and you sign a document to secure the loan by your inventory or other collateral. If you default on the loan they keep the collateral. But if you sell and make money you can pay it off quickly and use it again like a credit line. You can also consider creating an inventory financing arrangement with a business associate or even a family member.

CHAPTER 10

Providing Outstanding Customer Satisfaction

If you know anything about Amazon you know that they are known for their world class customer satisfaction. This is by far the biggest shingle that they hang outside of their door, and what they are known for. Their ability to honor customer's needs and provide them with the best quality customer satisfaction has caused them to be ranked highest among most marketplaces.

So, of course, if you start your Amazon selling business, Amazon will expect you to provide the same quality customer satisfaction that they do. Amazon will also support you and your customers in this, for they know that if you succeed then they do as well.

Let's consider the keys to great customer satisfaction. The keys to great customer satisfaction in Amazon include:

1. Sticking to the Golden rule of customer satisfaction.

2. Resolving customer issues quickly.

3. Extending the long-term value of your customers.

The Golden Rule of Customer Satisfaction

The golden rule of customer satisfaction is just like the Golden Rule, which is to treat your customers the way you would like to be treated. In other words, the treatment that you appreciate, your customers will appreciate. If you wouldn't cut corners with the quality of the products that you purchase, do not cut corners on the products you're going to be selling. If you don't see value in a particular product there's a good chance that your customers will not see the value as well. Or, if something comes in the wrong packaging and you don't feel good about it, it's a good chance your customers are going to feel the same. For example, if something is sent to you in generic packaging, with the product covered in bubble wrap, you will probably feel like it's cheap or a knock-off. Your customers are going to feel the same way if you send them a product in generic packaging and covered in bubble wrap.

So, the golden rule in Amazon is to treat your customers better than you would like to be treated yourself.

Resolving Customer Issues

You must expect customer issues to come up. Actually, look forward to them because it's an opportunity to get closer to your customers and connecting with them better. But when customer issues do come up, be ready to bend over backwards to help your customers be satisfied.

The loyalty of your customers is the lifeblood of your business, so you need to honor them as best as you can. For example, if you have a product that is consistently getting complaints, get rid of your product, and get a more high quality product. If you have a product that could benefit from adding an accessory, listen to your customers and provide the accessories your customers are asking for. Otherwise, they will go to your competitor, which will gladly give them what they want and need.

The idea is to make sure you're taking care of your customers and providing them with whatever needs they have. By doing this, they will reward you with more positive reviews, referrals, and more sales.

This also means being willing to sacrifice profit to help your customers get their needs met. For example, recently, I had a customer refund a product, and I offered him 50% coupon off his next purchase if he would come back. He returned in a matter of days. Now he is going to be my customer for a very long time.

Extending the Long Term Value of Your Customers

Customer long term value is the amount of purchases your customers make from you over a period of time. So, it will benefit you to get your customers to purchase from you again and again as long as possible.

The best ways to extend the long term value of your customers is to stay in the customer's mind even after they have purchased from you. One way to stay in the customer's mind is through email. Now you're probably thinking, "How am I supposed to get my customer's email, since Amazon guards their email with their life?" It is true. Amazon does not give up customer's emails. Yet there are ways you can still get your customer's emails and stay in their mind.

The key to getting customer's emails is in the bonus that you offer with your product. If you put a postcard offering a bonus inside of the package that goes to your customer, your customer will open it, and follow the directions on it to get their bonus. They will go to your website and put their information in the website form to get their free bonus. Then you can capture their email, and communicate to your customer from then on with different promotions to purchase your other products.

Another way to communicate with your customer is to correspond through the Amazon email system. In your emails you can add a phone number where they can contact you for questions. When they do call you, you can ask them for their email and add them to your database. I was able to capture the email and phone number of my first customer on Amazon, because he called me to answer a question he had about his product. From then on, I've been contacting him ever since.

Other ways to capture customer information is by telling them about more bonuses that they can get access to if they sign up for your newsletter. Again, that can be communicated to them through a little slip of paper you put in with the package you mail to them, directing them to sign up for your newsletter online. After you get their contact information, you can email them and tell them about any new promotions or accessories that you have. Or contact them on special occasions, like their birthday, or on a special holiday.

Another way to extend the long-term value of a customer is to provide them with a continuous supply of products that they can purchase. I'm talking about accessories, complimentary products from your competitors, or complimentary products you create. The idea is that you're consistently giving them new products that fit their needs, that they'll be interested in. If you don't have additional products, get them from your competitor at a discounted price. Or make an agreement with your competitor to provide it for you under your brand name.

Or you can provide a new product that you create. The same branding process that we talked about before works here too. Just find a great wholesale source that sells a great complimentary product, brand it, package it and sell it to your customers.

You can also create a membership for your customers. Contact them and let them know about the special membership that you offer, where they can get special promotions or different discounts for being part of that membership. Then sell them exclusive products made just for them.

CHAPTER 11

Getting Abundant Reviews

Now, let's talk about the lifeblood of your Amazon selling business, which is getting reviews. I really like getting reviews for my products. Why? Because I like to make sure that people are happy with the things that I sell. So I'm always either testing my product with people, asking people's feedback about my product, or asking them for reviews.

Reviews are the Holy Grail of your products, because they are, by far, the biggest thing that motivate risk-averse customers to purchase.

So, let's talk about how to get reviews with integrity. There are a lot of underhanded ways to get reviews that go against Amazon's policy. But I'm going to talk about how to do it the right way. The three most effective ways to get reviews are:

1. Get reviews from customers that have bought your product directly.

2. Ask for product testing reviews from non-paying customers.

3. Ask for product reviews from customers that buy the product via promotional or complimentary codes.

Getting Reviews from Paying Customers

The quickest and easiest way to get reviews is to get it from customers that have already bought your product. They have firsthand experience with your product and if they like your product they will be highly motivated to review.

Unfortunately, 10 percent of Amazon customers review. It's very different from eBay where customers give reviews all of the time. Because of this you need to proactively motivate customers to leave great reviews.

The best way to motivate customers to give you a review is to ask. Amazon makes this possible by allowing you to message your customers through the Amazon Seller Central Message center. They even give you the option of messaging customers to ask for reviews.

Therefore, one very critical part of your Amazon selling business is to send every customer a follow up email to ask for a review. This is the email that I send every customer within 14 days after they receive their product:

Dear < Customer Name Here >,

We hope that you are satisfied with your new < Product Name Here>.

We want to make sure that you are satisfied in every way, so again, if there is anything that we can do to help you, please let us know.

And if you feel satisfied with your product, and of the way you have been treated as a customer, your positive review on Amazon would be greatly appreciated.

To leave a quick review just click here: <Amazon Product review page URL here>

Thank you, again, for being our valued customer.

<Brand> Support Team
<Brand Name Here>

P.S.: If you need to reach us for any reason, please do not hesitate to email us through Amazon.

For every 50 customers, I can guarantee about 5—10 reviews through that email message alone.

The best part about this email is that I encourage them to contact me in case they have any issues. This gives me the opportunity to fix any problems or issues the customer has before they can leave a negative review.

The biggest benefits of getting paid customer reviews are that they are considered "verified purchase reviews" which carries more weight for other potential customers to purchase your product. Not all customers understand the difference between "verified purchase reviews" and non-verified reviews, but more and more customers are becoming aware of it. Therefore, it is important to get as many "verified purchase" reviews as you can to help motivate more savvy Amazon customers to buy.

Getting Reviews from Non-Paying Customers

Now, when you begin your Amazon Selling business or when you first list a product, it is difficult to get customer reviews, because you haven't sold anything yet. It is a catch 22, because you need reviews to get sales, but you need sales in order to ask for reviews. So what can you do to get out of product review limbo? The best solution is to get reviews from non-paying customers.

Amazon allows you to get reviews from non-paying customers by either giving them the product for free in exchange for an unbiased review, or by asking them to test the product and giving an unbiased review.

If you are in the testing phase of your product, you don't have much inventory to give away. Therefore your best bet is to get product test reviews from people that you know. This can be as simple as asking someone to test your product and give an unbiased review on your listing. The following process is the system I use to get as many product test reviews as I can during the testing phase:

1. Ask a friend or family member to test your product and to give you an unbiased review on Amazon.

2. Show them the product, and let them test it.

3. Use the opportunity to also ask them for valuable feedback on the product, that you can use to improve your product experience.

4. Get their email, and email them the instructions on how to review your product on Amazon. Add the link to the product review page as well.

5. Sit back and wait for the reviews to come in.

6. If they forget, send them a follow up email reminding them to review.

The more reviews you get, the more sales you will get. It's that simple. So try to get as many product test reviews during the test phase of your product.

Getting Reviews from Non-Paying Customers Through Complimentary Promotions

Another way to get reviews is to give your product away for free for an unbiased review of your product. Now, the easiest way to do this is to give your product away, then send an email to your product recipients with instructions on how to review. But an even more powerful way to do this is through COMP promotion codes you create on Amazon Seller Central.

Imagine this for a moment. You know a person in another state, that has agreed to give you an unbiased review in exchange for your free product. If you use FBA, the simplest way to get them the product is to create a COMP code in Amazon Seller Central, and send it to them. They then purchase the product through their Amazon account, using their COMP code to get it for free, and the product is automatically sent to them. Once they get the product, they test it and they then give you a review.

The indirect result of doing this is that the review will be considered a "verified purchase" review since it was purchased through Amazon, even though a COMP code was used. Also, Amazon registers this transaction as a sale, which also improves your sales rank, which results in more exposure for you.

Therefore, if you are going to give your product away for an unbiased review, make sure it goes through the Amazon purchasing system. Create a COMP code, give it to everyone you will be giving a free sample to, and have them purchase the item directly through Amazon. If you don't use FBA, you can ship the item to them directly. Or if you are in close proximity to the person, you can deliver the product to them. The most important thing is that the transaction is registered in Amazon as a sale.

Handling Negative Reviews

So how do you handle the dreaded negative review? The truth is that you will get negative reviews because you will be dealing with all types of customers, and you cannot control their responses. You can do everything right, and have the best product on the planet, but you will still find someone that will have something to complain about.

But how can you handle the negative reviews that will eventually come? Here are a few ways to deal with them:

1. **Dilute your negative reviews by having an abundance of positive reviews.**

   The good thing about Amazon is that reviews are based on averages. The combination of all of your reviews are added together then divided by the amount of reviews you have. For example, if you have 20 five-star reviews and two two-star reviews then you will get a review score of four and a half stars or maybe even a five-star overall review, because Amazon will average it out.

So it is imperative that you get as many positive four to five star reviews as you can. It is also important to continue week after week getting four to five star reviews, for the life of the product. All of the positive reviews will dilute any negative reviews that will occasionally show up.

2. **Communicate with the buyer, fix their problem and ask for a new review.**

Sometimes you may want to try to communicate with the buyer through the Amazon Seller Central messaging service to see if you can resolve the problem. If you can resolve the problem or if you can reimburse the customer for any problems they experienced, you can then request the customer to re-review your product. When you do ask, you need to ask gently and humbly, or the customer may feel like they are being badgered by you, which you want to avoid.

Also, consider that maybe the customer was expressing an accurate flaw in your product, that you may not know of. In this case, the negative review is your friend, and because of this you need to begin every correspondence with your customer by thanking them for the review, whether negative or positive. Remember, the only feedback you can count on is the feedback you get from customers, so approach your customers this way, and you may be able to work with them to fix the issue. Also, customers are more apt to re-review your product after you have made changes that they suggest.

CHAPTER 12

Automating Your Amazon Selling Business

We've talked about many things in this book, but wouldn't it be nice to be able to automate your entire Amazon Selling Business, so that you only have to work at it five to ten hours a month?

Well, there are many different resources you can use both through Amazon and outside of Amazon to greatly simplify and automate your Amazon Selling business. This includes automating:

1. The product selection process,

2. The product sourcing process,

3. The branding process,

4. Creating high converting Amazon listings process,

5. The fulfillment and inventory management process,

6. The customer satisfaction process, and

7. The review gathering process.

The idea is, that in each of these areas, you can automate each process so you save a lot of the extra time, effort, resources, and money you would normally use, but still continue to create a lot of revenue, income and profit.

Automating the Product Selection Process

One way you to automate the product selection process is by taking the product selection process I mentioned in the early parts of this book, and use it to train a virtual assistant to find ideal potential products for you, using your criteria. You can show them the step by step process, or you can make a video of the process, and then have them focus on finding products week per week in every category you are interested in. This way all you have to do is to review the products they find to see which is the best one for your to pursue.

You can find great virtual assistants on Elance.com or Odesk. com. You can even find a good assistant for $5 on Fiverr.com. Or you can get an intern from the local college to do it for you.

Automating the Sourcing Process

Just like the product selection process, you can train your virtual assistant on how to source products using the process I mentioned in the product sourcing chapter of this book. They can go through Alibaba and AliExpress looking for great suppliers, and they can email the suppliers the sourcing questions. They can follow up on any correspondence with suppliers, and even request for samples from qualified suppliers. If you trust your assistant, you can even give them access to a petty cash account through a debit or credit card with a limit, and have them order samples for you. You will do the sample testing yourself, but if you train your assistant well, they may be able to do this as well.

You can even find a virtual assistant in China, that specializes in finding high quality product sources in China, as well as has expertise in importing products from China. Elance.com is again a great source for finding professionals that offer this service.

Automating the Branding Process

For branding, you have the option to hire a branding specialist to help you come up with a great brand. It may be a small investment on your part, but the profitable result will justify the expense. Also you can go to Fiverr.com to find a graphic designer to help design your logo, packaging, etc.

Automating The Creation of High Converting Amazon Listings

You can find great people who specialize in Amazon listings. You can even find great copywriters that will apply their skills to your Amazon listing and get you great results. Personally, I have found some great Amazon Listing copywriters on Fiverr.com, and for $20 I was able to get a compelling title, bullets and description written for me for each product I have.

You also have the option of hiring an Amazon listing creation service. These are service providers that will design the entire Amazon product listing for you from scratch including: Titles, bullets, description, images, etc. Though they are a bit more expensive, (anywhere from $100.00 to $500.00) it will be a good return on investment, especially if you're making thousands of dollars in revenue.

Automating the Fulfilment and Inventory Management Process

To automate the fulfillment and management process there is no greater solution than Fulfillment by Amazon (FBA). FBA is just the easiest, most cost effective way to do it, because Amazon has the entire fulfillment process down to a science.

FBA will store, pick, pack, and ship your inventory. They will notify you via email if your inventory is running low. They handle all customer service questions and any returns. They also provide all types of reports, to let you project your inventory needs. Not to mention they provide you with all types of support and tools to help you succeed. It truly is a no brainer.

In addition to using FBA, you can automate your fulfillment and inventory management even further by either training your supplier to ship directly to Amazon FBA for you; by hiring a third party fulfillment center to receive your products, prepare them and send them to FBA; or by hiring an independent contractor to do it for you.

FBA has specific requirements to receive shipments to their warehouses. After you have confirmed the quality of the supplier's product, you can train your supplier to fulfill the Amazon shipping requirements and then send your product directly to Amazon. You can email them all of the product labels, and shipping labels as well. By doing this you will automate 95 percent of your entire Amazon Selling business. Just make sure you keep tabs on the quality of the product, by responding quickly to customer feedback or messaging customers to make sure they are satisfied.

If you cannot get your supplier to agree to do this, you can hire a third party fulfillment service that will receive your products from your supplier, package them and then send it to Amazon for you.

Usually this type of service cost a few cents per product, but the extra time it frees up for you is worth the expense.

As a last resort, you can hire an independent contractor to receive, prepare and ship your product to Amazon. You will need to have a well-documented system, provide them limited access to your Amazon Seller Central Account, and train them thoroughly. After they have proven themselves you can incentivize them with a higher salary or bonuses. The benefit of using an independent contractor is that you can also train them to test each product for quality, guaranteeing that you only send your customers the highest quality products.

Automating The Customer Satisfaction Process

How do you automate the customer satisfaction process? Personally, I have pre-prepared emails to go out to my customers for different events in the buying process. For example, right after they purchase they get an email from me through the Amazon messaging service telling them "Welcome, I'm grateful you're here, this is when your product is going to be sent out, I'm looking forward to working with you," etc. So, it lets them know from the beginning what they can expect from us in terms of customer service.

Then, right after it ships out I let them know, "Hey, your item has shipped, it's on its way, get ready for it." If shipping takes a little longer than usual, which may happen, I'll send an email saying, "Hey, just to let you know this is when it's coming..." The key is to keep the customer in the loop.

I also send an email right after the product arrives, requesting a review. Sometimes, I even send a postcard. But I have all of these emails and materials as templates prepared beforehand to go out immediately at different points. And, if you want to automate this further, a virtual assistant can be trained to send these out at appropriate times.

As for customer inquiries, you can have your virtual assistant respond to all customer inquiries and issues. Just train them to know exactly what to do, and to have the right attitude dealing with the customer so they're actually friendly, kind, and serviceable. Once this is done, the entire customer service process is automated and you don't have to do much of anything. Then all you have to do is collect a check. And if you use FBA, Amazon does all this for you.

Automating the Review Gathering Process

To automate the review gathering process it's good to have a list of people you can approach right away, to test any new products you list, that are also trained to give reviews. Also, it's wise to set aside a certain number units of your inventory to give away for free to get reviews. Have email templates prepared to go out to customers reminding them to give a review. Also, have inserts to go in your packaging to remind customers to give a review as well. The idea is that throughout the purchasing process they're reminded to give a review over and over, and if they have a great experience, they generally will.

You can outsource the sending out of emails to customers asking for reviews, to a virtual assistant also. They can do it on a weekly basis, sending your customer review template to new customers within 14 days of their purchase. This gives you a great edge in the Amazon marketplace because other sellers on Amazon rarely do this.

CHAPTER
13

Growing and Expanding Your Amazon Selling Business

Let's now talk about how to scale your Amazon business. In other words, how to expand your Amazon Selling business and sell more or new products.

One of the best options to expand your Amazon business is to go deep, and then go wide. In other words, go deep by selling the most you can in your own product category, and then go wide by testing out new products in new, unrelated categories.

Go Deep, First...

It's always good to go deep first because that way you will master one product or product line. You've done the testing and validating. You also know your customers well, because you've dealt with them, and you understand them. And if you apply all that you've learned in this book, you will dominate in your product category.

For example, if you're selling a particular type of wine accessory, you have the option to sell many more types of wine accessories. You can also sell complimentary products like a book on wine tasting, or a wine storage unit. Next thing you know, you're selling multiple wine accessory products at the same time, sometimes to multiple customers, or even to the same customer. You're now making money in a very expanded, scaled way.

...Then, Go Wide!

The next step toward the growth of your Amazon selling business is to go wide. In other words, selling into different product lines and different product categories. This means selling completely different products altogether because you see a great opportunity in another category. For example, you can be very successful selling wine stoppers and then succeed selling cupcake liners as well.

But, in order to go wide you're going to have to go through the entire Amazon process again, in order to master your new product. But, by then, you will have the process down to a science, and the profits from your efforts will be well worth it. Soon you'll have ten or twenty products in different product lines or categories bringing you a substantial income.

CHAPTER

14

The Amazon Selling Secrets 90 Day Action Plan

In this chapter I have provided a step by step, 90 Day Plan of Action that will help you to get even closer to your goal of making $1K—$10K a month selling your own products on Amazon. This is the process I have and many others have used, and if you stick to it, you will more guarantee your success.

You can follow the plan exactly, or go faster if you like. But its best to commit to achieving each of the weekly goals in order to see progress in your Amazon Selling business.

Preparation

1. Go through Entire "Amazon Selling Secrets" book from cover to cover.

2. Get $1K–$2K in capital or credit to start with. If you can't get that much, try to get at least $500 to start with.

3. Reserve 5–10 hours a week to work on your Amazon Business.

   1. Either a few hours every day or use your weekends.

4. Open an Individual Amazon Seller Central Account.

   1. Go to: http://services.amazon.com/content/sell-on-amazon.htm

5. Follow all of the next steps.

Week 1: Identify The Product You Will Sell

1. Set Criteria for your product (use my list from this book or create your own).

2. Go through the Amazon Bestseller Research Process and find 10–20 potential products.

3. Run your numbers using the Amazon Profit Calculator, and make sure the price/ expense of your products make sense to reach your profit goal.

   1. To Download the Amazon Profit/ Cost Calculator go to www.Amazonsellingsecretsbook.com/cost-calculator.

4. Research all product competitors to identify their strengths, weaknesses, opportunities and threats (SWOT).

1. Check all of your competitor's Amazon reviews for more information (Focus on reviews that are rated 3 stars or less).
5. Pick your final 5—10 potential products.

Week 2: Source Your Product and Order Samples

1. Open an Aliexpress and Alibaba Account.
2. Go through Aliexpress find 10—30 suppliers to source products and product prices.

   1. Send the sourcing questions.
3. Go through Alibaba for additional 10—30 suppliers to source products and look for better product prices.

   1. Send sourcing questions.
4. Pick final 5—10 potential suppliers.
5. Order samples from suppliers. (If samples are inexpensive, order 5 at a time).

Week 3: Create Your Brand and USP

1. Pick Brand name (s) to sell product under.
2. Pick Product USP(s).
3. Research more competitors and competitor reviews.
4. Pick product Name (s).
5. Get Brand Logo from Fiverr.com.

Week 4: Receive Samples and Order Test Products

1. Receive samples and test thoroughly.

2. Get feedback for samples from others.

3. Make decision on final product and final wholesale supplier you will use.

4. Order 5—10 Products for Testing from your final supplier.

Week 5: Go Live—Create Listing and Test the Product in the Amazon Marketplace

1. Go to Fiverr.com and pay copywriter to create product Description listing, or write it yourself.

2. Create title and bullet description for product (you can have copywriter do this, but I usually do it myself).

3. Choose Pictures—Get pictures either from supplier, or stock photo. Go to Fiverr.com to enhance photos.

4. Choose Pricing for your product.

5. Create your Product Listing.

6. Use one sample for different people to product test and ask them for reviews.

Week 6: Tweak The Product Listing Until You Get Daily Sales. Test Your Sourcing Process. Get Reviews

1. Tweak your title, and rotate pictures until you start seeing sales.

2. Reduce price daily, until you get daily sales.

3. Calculate new prices using the Amazon Price/Cost Calculator. Check to see if the changed daily sales price is acceptable.

4. Fulfill Orders for customers manually (later you can convert to FBA).

5. Establish rapport with customers with internal Messaging through Amazon.

6. Review your entire sourcing process with your supplier to see if it is acceptable.

7. Request any changes from supplier that are necessary.

Week 7: Order Bulk Inventory

1. Order minimum order quantity (MOQ) bulk inventory with your logo from your supplier. (obtain credit or cash as necessary to pay for it).

2. Order packaging with logo (whether from supplier, or packing printing company, etc.).

3. Create inserts to go in packages.

Week 8: Send Inventory to FBA.
Get More Reviews

1. Buy boxes to send product to FBA.

2. Select FBA Inventory Placement option (In case you desire your products go to one warehouse).

3. Prepare and print all labels for products and shipment to FBA.

4. Ship to FBA.

5. Wait till products are received and stored in FBA inventory.

6. Convert all inventory listings to "Fulfillment By Amazon."

7. Give different people (product testers) promo code so they can get free samples by purchasing product for free through Amazon, and giving a verified review (for sales rank too).

Week 9: Tweak Pricing to Get Best Seller
Status or First Page Bestseller Position.
Get More Reviews

1. Tweak price daily to get to bestseller status.

2. Check to make sure profit margins are still acceptable.

3. Check results once a day.

4. Use Test Stock to send to people product for free (using promo comp codes) to get more reviews.

Week 10: Create an Inventory Management Process

1. Prep to order inventory once every month or every 3 months.

2. Create Inventory Management Calendar to determine inventory needs and cash needed.

3. Renegotiate rates and terms with supplier to lessen expense.

4. *(Optional)* Train Supplier to send to FBA, or hire independent contractor to receive and prep inventory, or hire fulfillment company (I.e.: Myinventoryteam.com).

Week 11: Review all processes and tweak for improvement

Week 12: Set Your Amazon Selling business on complete autopilot and go look for new products

CHAPTER
15
Conclusion

In conclusion, with the Amazon selling process that you've learned in this book you can begin to make anywhere from $1,000 to $10,000 a month on Amazon. If you follow the specific direction in this book step by step, it's only a matter of time before you create your own automated passive income stream in as little as 90 days. Personally, I started making money within the first month that I started this process. But on average, you can expect to see results within the first three months.

So, if you can gather a little capital to start, and use it wisely; If you follow the steps that I gave you in identifying products, identifying suppliers, creating a powerful brand, creating high converting listings and getting abundant reviews; and if you test and validate everything; it's almost guaranteed that you will be able to make anywhere from $1,000 to $10,000 a month, and create a second income for yourself.

But it does take dedication, because there is a learning curve. It takes determination, to keep going until you are successful. It takes patience, because maybe the first product will not be a winner. But don't forget, that's the way it's supposed to be. You are going to keep testing and tweaking until you make it work for you.

So, your dedication, your determination and your patience will bring you success. Most importantly, in the end, it will pay off because you will create a great passive income stream for you and your family to enjoy.

It's been a pleasure bringing this Amazon Selling System to you. And, if you need more help, you can try my Amazon Selling Secrets Video Training Program on Udemy.com on the link below. It gives you more detailed training and resources to help you become a successful Amazon Seller. And as a reward for getting this far, if you use coupon Code AmazonSuccess49, you can get the course for 75% OFF.

For the Amazon Video Course—"Make $1K—$10K a Month Selling Your Own Products on Amazon" Video Course—go to

www.udemy.com/how-to-make-an-extra-1k-10k-
a-month-selling-on-amazon

Good luck and God bless,
William U. Peña, MBA

Appendix A

Resources

Identifying Profitable Products
Profit Spotlight—profitspotlight.org

Sourcing from China
China Importal—www.chinaimportal.com
Proven China Sourcing (Paid service—but very useful)—
provenchinasourcing.com

Automating Your Amazon Business
Daniel J from "A Slice of the Pie" has put together a great blog on
how to automate sourcing, receiving and having either your assistant
or the wholesaler/manufacturer to ship items directly to FBA.—
http://alittlesliceofthepie.com/

Amazon FBA
Amazon FBA Training YouTube Playlists—
www.youtube.com/user/FulfillmentbyAmazon/playlists

Sales Taxes for US Amazon Sellers

Since the best tax advice will come from Tax Professionals, I have added a link to one of the most knowledgeable companies that understand the ins and outs of sales tax requirements for US Amazon sellers.—www.TaxJar.com

Disclaimer: I am not a tax professional, this is for educational purposes only.

www.ingramcontent.com/pod-product-compliance
Lightning Source LLC
Chambersburg PA
CBHW071711210326
41597CB00017B/2429